trotman

HOW TO WRITE A WINNING UCAS PERSONAL STATEMENT

IAN STANNARD

The Daily Telegraph

How to Write a Winning UCAS Personal Statement

This first edition published in 2008 by Trotman Publishing, a division of Crimson Publishing Ltd., Westminster House, Kew Road, Richmond, Surrey TW9 2ND

© Trotman Publishing 2008

Reprinted 2009

Author: Ian Stannard

Designed by Andy Prior

British Library Cataloguing in Publication Data
A catalogue record for this book is available from the British Library

ISBN 978-1-84455-180-4

Typeset by Newgen Imaging Systems Pvt Ltd.
Printed and bound in Great Britain by Bell & Bain Ltd, Glasgow

HOW TO WRITE A WINNING UCAS PERSONAL STATEMENT

Contents

PREFACE

It has been a privilege to work so closely with hundreds of young aspiring undergraduates over the last decade. Education reforms have come and gone, yet the essential principles of success remain the same. If you work hard at what you enjoy, take care to present yourself enthusiastically and articulately, and take the time to think about what you want from life, you will not go far wrong. Applying to university is not an exact science. Choices about where to study, what to study and whether to study are essentially personal. These personal choices will be influenced by your parents' aspirations, your background, your friends and your teachers. However, when push comes to shove, the choices you make are your own and your need to take responsibility for them.

You therefore need to be informed. This information also needs to be informed by current experience and reality, not 'what it was like in my day'! This is the purpose of this book and why I felt moved to write it. It will help you write a good personal statement and so present a good winning application to a university admissions panel. The advice in it is current and – importantly – driven by the experts, the admissions tutors who will read your application. They are the 'gatekeepers' who ultimately decide your fate. It is their views that count most in this competitive process.

My own views have been coloured by working at one the UK's ancient schools, Christ's Hospital, for the last decade or so. Although it is an independent school, with able students, it remains one of the few 'needs blind' public schools in the UK. If we assess that like a pupil has potential for greater things, we take that pupil and ask the parents to pay a fee that is commensurate with their ability to pay, which means that some may pay nothing. This is because the school is allied to one of the oldest educational charities in the UK and still remains true to its ethos, an ethos that was developed during the reign of Edward VI. As a result I teach pupils from all walks of life. Some are first-time applicants from their family to seek higher education and tick all the widening participation boxes. Others are sons or daughters of Oxford graduates who bring their own unique problems to solve.

This mix has meant that I have dealt with the full range of issues that can arise in this area and have an idea what it is students and parents new to this process want and need to know. The personal statement is for many the scariest part of the application. It need not be so and this book will help to ease you through this part of the form so that you end up with something of which you can be proud.

PART ONE
INTRODUCTION

❛ The personal statement is a crucial part of the UCAS form: a marketing tool for your interests, talents, and accomplishments. ❜

QUEEN MARY'S, UNIVERSITY OF LONDON

The personal statement is probably the most important piece of writing that most students aiming to gain entry in higher education will complete outside of an examination hall. In an increasingly competitive marketplace, the supply of good courses in many areas of study is outstripped by demand. The result is that for some highly competitive courses, such as psychology, medicine, law, English and physiotherapy the number of applicants can exceed supply by ten times.

Most universities do not have the resources to interview all good candidates. They rely principally on four pieces of information when deciding whether to offer the applicant a place:

1 The student's academic record so far and their current academic profile – are they studying A levels, International Baccalaureate or an equivalent qualification?

2 The student's personal statement

3 The academic reference provided by the school or college

4 The predicted grades that the school or college provide.

My experience of talking to many current admissions tutors is that they look first at the academic record and personal statement. They do look at predicted grades and the academic reference, but increasingly they base their opinion on the actual GCSE and AS grades achieved to date and the quality of the personal statement. Since the decision was made to make the academic reference 'open' rather than confidential, the references that were once candid are now increasingly bland or unwilling to say anything that might undermine the success of an application.

This point is tellingly made in a comment received from an admissions tutor at Nottingham University:

> We are somewhat concerned about some tutors overselling their students, exaggerating their predicted grades and abilities of the candidate so as to get them a good university place. Where the expected performance can be demonstrated or justified (for example, with overall grades or an upward trajectory in performance) the student's case is improved. This is especially important where predicted performance and current or previous performance appear to differ.

Therefore – wake up and smell the coffee!

It is hard to get a place at a good university and it is therefore vital that you follow these basic rules of thumb:

Your UCAS application must be handed in on time and be free from errors: There is a school of thought that says that an early application gives an applicant an edge. This depends on the policy of the university. Some offer places throughout the application cycle (normally September to mid-January) and others operate what is known as a 'gathered field' approach and wait until the closing date. However, in my experience most will offer a good candidate a place as soon as they read the application. So an early application cannot do any harm.

Your personal statement must sell you in a way that is compelling, engaging and well informed: A lazy approach to this key document is fatal, particularly if you are applying to a course that is oversubscribed. A busy admissions tutor is looking for a reason to reject you as much as to offer you a place! In the real world, tutors will face a large pile of applications knowing that they are going to have to whittle them down to a shortlist. Don't give them an excuse to bin yours because of a poor statement.

Your reasons for applying must be good: Your statement must point to evidence that indicates that you understand the course content and have the skills to thrive in their department. This means taking time to do the research properly before doing anything else. You cannot write a winning application and statement without understanding your enemy!

It is a myth that the statement is the hardest thing to write, although in my experience it is what causes 50% of the heartache. The other 50% is deciding what to study and where. Making decisions is tough and for many of you this is the first time you will be making a major educational decision without your parents being at the centre of the process. You should consider their advice, together with the advice gained from books such as this, your teachers, university prospectuses and your friends. However, in the end it is you who sign and send the form to UCAS. You must therefore take responsibility for its success and failure.

Do not despair. I am a strong believer in the phrase 'Keep It Simple Stupid' or KISS for short! This is the purpose of this book. I aim to make the process of deciding what and where to study **and** writing your statement, less painful and more fulfilling. I have worked with thousands of students applying to universities all over the UK and have read more personal statements than I care to admit. If you follow the advice in this book, you will be well on the way to producing a statement and application that will win you the offer you want.

CHAPTER ONE
NO SHORT CUTS!

ou cannot write a good personal statement in isolation. The information you need to write it well is only gathered by careful research. This takes time but it is time well spent.

Think of the what, why and where questions that we often ask ourselves. You need to find out what you want to study, why this subject motivates you and then consider where you want to study. A common theme in all the conversations I have had with admissions tutors is that four things are vital:

- That you know what you really want from a university course
- That you can sell your enthusiasm for the subject you have chosen clearly and with confidence
- That you know what academic grades the departments are looking for – be brave but also realistic
- That the location you choose suits your personality and wider interests.

This is where the academic profiles (starting on page 61) will be so useful to you. Each one takes a different subject area and lets you know what studying that subject may be like, the qualities they look for in a good candidate, what to write and what to avoid in your personal statement and other tips to make your application stand out from the crowd. These were all written in collaboration with real admissions tutors and therefore do represent an inside guide to how to impress a busy academic tutor.

Here are some extracts from a range of subjects to whet your appetite!

This is what a tutor at Queen Mary's, University of London has to say about the skills or attributes that they look for in a good applicant for English:

❝ Admissions tutors will always consider the level of attainment in GCSEs and predicted grades for A levels first of all. Many English courses now demand very high grades, simply due to supply and demand. It is not at all uncommon for candidates to be made offers of AAB or higher. Equally, it is not unusual for candidates to be rejected from one or more of their preferred universities. However, it is also possible to get into English courses with lower grades. Do your research carefully! ❞

The personal statement and school reference are then read for any signs that interest in English is not just a narrow product of quite enjoying it at A level. Tutors would hope to see indications of longstanding enjoyment, and an understanding that English at university will not be like three more years of A level English, but will be more demanding and unpredictable. We want to see evidence of wide reading and an appreciation of different literary genres.

Good applicants demonstrate excellent academic potential, demonstrated by their strong A level or equivalent grades, and enthusiasm for further study. They show good time management and teamwork skills; the one to manage independent study successfully, the other to work co-operatively in seminars and group projects.'

All this information needs to be included in your personal statement or academic reference!

Here are some comments on what makes for a good personal statement for a potential physiotherapist from an admissions tutor at Brighton University.

❝ It's really helpful if you have observed some physiotherapy sessions, to briefly describe your experience and explain why you would like to study it. You really need to describe something more varied than a personal experience of receiving physiotherapy – which shows that you have made an effort to see different aspects of physiotherapy – or at least have plans to broaden your understanding. Many departments do not look favourably at an overemphasis on sport. Most physiotherapists work in hospital settings and do not get involved in any form of sports related injury or rehabilitation. *

It's always good to hear about your activities beyond the academic, particularly if you are interested in continuing them at university. Try and show a range of interests other than sport. We are interested in music, drama and other extracurricular pursuits, especially if they show evidence of individual leadership or teamwork skills. If you have had a job or done voluntary work make sure you explain something positive about the experience of interacting with people. *

Try and find a balance between self-promotion, explaining your recent experiences of work, social activities and school achievements. Overemphasis on any of these elements can skew your statement. *

You can read an example of a successful personal statement in Part Two.

SUMMARY

A good personal statement is one that is written at the end of an exhaustive research process. Students who are right for the course, who have understood the demands of the subject and are ready to take on the challenge write winning personal statements.

Weak personal statements are under-prepared, written in a hurry and without the zeal that is evident when an applicant knows what they want and promotes themselves with confidence.

Before you even start to write your personal statement you need to ask yourself some searching questions and be prepared to work hard to find the answers. Good applications are often successful applications, and successful applications are informed and enhanced by good research.

What I mean by this is that when you send in your application, it is sent on the assumption that you consent to UCAS passing it on. This consent implies that **you** have done your research and not relied on hearsay! Too many students drop out of university in their first year or change their course when they arrive, because they were poorly informed from the outset. This is crucial, not least, because it is expensive to go to university and you don't want to waste your money!

Informed consent is not easy! You need to devote a considerable amount of time to this process to prepare a winning application and personal statement. The bulk of a personal statement is a clear, convincing and enthusiastic statement of why you are passionate about that subject you wish to read at university. This passion and enthusiasm is hard to muster without a clear vision of what it is that you are letting yourself in for!

One good way to start is to answer these questions – make notes that you can refer back to later when we start to draft your statement.

QUESTIONS TO ASK YOURSELF

Why do you want to study that subject and what evidence do you have that your interest is real and not superficial?	This is a key component of the first part of your personal statement.
Where do you want to study and why?	Admissions tutors want to know that your reasons for studying a subject at their university are based on good grounds. Do you understand the demands of the course or the type of

teaching and learning styles that you will encounter? This is something that ought to be addressed in a statement.

What do you know about the skills and attributes that the admissions tutor is looking for and how will you convince them that you possess these key skills?

Emphasise these skills in your statement.

What evidence can you provide that supports your interest? This evidence must be more than just a list of what you have done at A level.

A good personal statement will show evidence of wider reading or participation in activities that support and extend your knowledge and understanding of the course you have applied for.

What do admissions tutors in your area of interest look for in a good statement?

Go to the profile section first and if in doubt, email or telephone a tutor at a local university for advice. They are keen to hear from potential applicants, particularly those local to the applicant's home.

What have your studies so far taught you about the course you hope to apply for – for instance, if applying to read Chemistry, what have you done at A level or equivalent that sparked your interest?

This is another key part of your personal statement and may be included in the first or second section.

What extracurricular activities do you undertake – do any of them give evidence of personal leadership, excellence or initiative?	This is what you write in the final part of a good personal statement.
What plans do you have post-graduation or are you planning a gap year?	This is something that you may allude to in the final section of your statement.

As you can see, there is a lot to think about before you start your first draft. I will start by asking you some questions about your motivation to study; your subject interests and what skills you have that you hope to extend at university. I will ask some searching questions that you may like to discuss with your family, friends or schoolteachers. I will also point you in the direction of some excellent books, websites and organisations that may help you in this initial process.

Only when you can answer all these questions are you ready to start the drafting stage. I suggest that you divide your statement into three distinct parts, working on each and then drawing them together at the end. Each part has its own emphasis and importance and a chapter of the book is devoted to each part in turn.

We start with some advice about research – why to do it, how to do it and where to look for expert help and guidance.

CHAPTER TWO
WHY GO TO UNIVERSITY IN THE FIRST PLACE?

In your parents' lifetime, the number of students in full time education post-18 has risen significantly. The government wants 50% of the British population to attend higher education – this is far higher than the figures that attended in the past. In the 1980s, less than 20% of the population attended a British university. The increase in demand has brought with it its own problems. In the 1980s there was a large grant cheque at the start of the term for many, most students would eat well in the college refectory and drink enormous quantities of beer in the college bar. As soon as the money started to run out it was soup and a roll in the refectory and a beer that lasted all evening!

The only way to secure more money was the benevolent bank manager, and students who went overdrawn, as most students did without parental support, were not always given extended credit! It was rare to see students with multiple store cards and credit cards. There were few hardship funds, access to learning funds and no advice and guidance on budgeting; equally there were no tuition fees either.

The debts and the numbers of students going to university were small but rewards were high to this élite. Because of the limited supply of graduates, employers were making highly attractive offers to students, and unemployment after graduation was unheard of. It was a huge incentive to go to university and apart from modest borrowing from the bank or parents to supplement the grant cheque, the loss of income when compared with those going straight into employment after A levels was soon recouped from much higher starting salaries.

Today the financial implications of going to university and completing a three- or four-year course, is a serious issue calling for full and proper consideration and consultation before you make the commitment.

UNIVERSITY TODAY

The drive to increase the numbers entering higher education has resulted in sustained growth of degree places during the past 20 years, students have to pay for their education and when they graduate, it is becoming more difficult to obtain the higher paid graduate jobs that were the norm before.

From October 2006 all students who wish to study in the UK have been required to pay tuition fees of up to £3,145. The only group who are exempt from this new initiative are students living in Scotland who pay no fees if they take a degree in Scotland. Loans and grants are the principal source of information and most students will leave university with considerable debts.

A student studying in London for three years and claiming all the loans available will run up debts of over £28,000! But they will only have to repay this money, on easy terms, when they secure a job earning over £15,000 per year.

For more information about student finance

UCAS website (www.ucas.ac.uk/students/studentfinance/)

Ian Stannard and Godfrey Cooper, *A 6th Former's Guide to Money Matters*, ZigZag Education Publishers, www.Zigzageducation.co.uk

SO WHY GO?

Essentially the reasons for this are varied and these are some of the factors that students I have worked with have come up with:

- **To get a good job:** most professional careers now have a recognised graduate entry route. Although it is not imperative to get a degree to get a good job, there is an assumption that graduates are more likely to be employed. Of course, once you start your career, your success or otherwise will depend on your ability to **do** the job. A degree is just the key to the door; it does not always guarantee that you will enjoy accelerated promotion.
- **To please my parents:** many parents live vicariously through their children. In my experience they vary in their approach. Some parents are too pushy and expect their children to go to university, as this was their own experience. This is particularly true of parents who expect their child

to get a place at Oxbridge or medical school. Others are equally forceful about the need to get a degree, especially as non-graduates themselves, they realise the advantages of a degree in career progression.

- **All my friends are applying:** this is another powerful pull towards university. This is particularly the case when the student's friends all aspire to higher education.

- **To better myself:** this group of students want to go to university to help them enjoy a better life than their parents were able to give them. Evidence does suggest that the most successful students at university will often be those that had to fight hard to get in, perhaps against the odds, for a variety of social or educational reasons. The **Widening Participation** model was established to work with and encourage this cohort of students.

- **I am not sure what I want to do for a living:** some students go to university to put off the inevitable life choice. They are unsure of what they want to do, so they go to university to give them more time to consider their options.

- **My chosen career requires me to graduate:** many degree courses, for example medicine, nursing, engineering, law, physiotherapy and veterinary science, are vocational and a degree qualification is an essential first step.

- **To make more money:** this is the most mercenary of all the motives but probably lies at the heart of most students' thoughts when contemplating three more years in education. Recent estimates suggest that graduates earn up to £300,000 more than non graduates over the course of a working lifetime of 30 to 40 years.

PAUSE FOR THOUGHT

You need to ask some more questions and take notes of your answers to refer back to later on. These questions are often best debated with friends, family and teachers at your school or college. Don't be afraid to ask the opinions of others to help inform your own.

These are all important questions to answer **before** you start to write your personal statement. They force you to look at yourself critically and assess the real reason you want to stay in full time education or perhaps not, and take some time out.

Do you look forward to leaving school and beginning in higher education?

Leaving school can be an exciting and scary prospect. The certainties of school and college life are lost. You are used to a group of friends that you may have known for years, rules you understand (even if you hate them!), teachers who you understand how to manipulate and teaching styles that you are used to. Starting again in a new institution, away from home for the first time and with all the bills to pay yourself can be daunting! Do not be afraid to express these fears and talk them through. You are not alone – far from it!

Do you want to continue to study a subject that you are studying at school or college?

Most students study a subject at university that is in some way linked to their educational choices post-16. Even if you are not studying the subject directly, such as English, chemistry or maths, many will choose a discipline that builds on skills learnt at A level (or their equivalent) for instance biochemistry or nursing, which both build on science skills learnt at school. This is important to consider when choosing the course.

How will you show this transfer of skills in your personal statement?

Going to university is also the opportunity to do other subjects that you are interested to explore but may not have done before. Subjects such as archaeology, classics, philosophy, law, podiatry and management are open to you in a way that they may not have been at school. Here, the admissions tutors are not looking for evidence of existing A level knowledge, just potential and latent interest. For example, the classics tutor at King's College London makes it clear that they do not look for classics or Latin at A level but rather for skills picked up in most humanities or language courses:

> As a good Classics (etc) applicant you will have the same general skills and attributes as any good humanities prospect: enthusiasm, self-motivation, a desire to learn, an appetite both for different perspectives and for challenging questions. The King's College London admissions team hope to see applicants who enjoy

independently exploring new topics, whether in the library, the museum, or the field; people who want to engage with new problems and techniques, and to get behind the clichés of mass-media versions of ancient myth and conflict. **,**

Do you want to live away from home?

Unlike in mainland Europe, UK students have traditionally moved away from home to study post-18. This is a trend that seems to be in modest decline, with an increasing number of students choosing to live in their home town. This is particularly true of undergraduates from poorer families with little history of higher education. Reasons for this vary, but the financial advantage of home life is one major factor.

Are you willing to pay for this opportunity and what is your attitude to debt?

It is not cheap to study at university. There are a number of costs that need to be met and for most students there is a shortfall between the income they receive from grants, bursaries and loans and the total cost of living. However, the advantages of a university degree are significant and money should not put anyone off giving it a try. Do consider the cost of living when looking at location. It is far more expensive to live and study in London than Hull! You will learn to live in debt as a student but this is quite manageable if you follow some simple tips:

- **Learn to budget:** look at your outgoings (spending habits) and look at your income. As much as possible try not to leave too big a gap between the two.
- **Avoid credit cards and store cards:** these are often a disaster for students and can lead to major problems, including court action, if you cannot make the payments. I know more than one former student who cannot get a mortgage now because of credit card debt when they were at university. This is real life now, not school rules and detentions!
- Expect to have to **get a job** in term time and in the holidays.
- Keep a check on your **spending on luxuries**, including alcohol and fast food. Try to learn to cook for yourself as this is almost always cheaper than precooked microwave meals. It is also sometimes cheaper to live in catered halls as the food is provided for you. As long as you eat it, this will cut your bills!

- Avoid unnecessary expenditure such as **car insurance**. Cars at university rarely make sense unless absolutely necessary. You become a taxi service!
- Make sure that you have personal insurance away from home and that you get a TV licence if you have a TV in your room. A hefty bill after a fire, or a fine after a visit from the TV licence van is not in most students' budget plans!

A small number of my former students have made all these mistakes in the last few years. For good advice, consult one of the many good guides to student money available in the shops or online.

Are you an independent learner?

The learning and teaching style at school is very different from that at university. There is a lot more emphasis on personal learning and initiative. This lack of direction and teacher contact is often a major source of disappointment for new undergraduates. Admissions tutors are looking for evidence in the personal statement that you have the drive and personal initiative to cope in this sort of environment. To give you an example, here is an extract from a profile written by admissions tutors at Surrey University and Durham University, both of which admit students into modern language courses.

Most language courses are taught using a variety of different methods. Some lectures are conducted either in English or a foreign language. These would normally be lectures to support modules in history, business or law for instance. They would also see students in small seminars, where the language was spoken and discussions take place about literature, politics or current affairs. Students are also encouraged to give presentations in the foreign language. Departments also use language laboratories and audiovisual material, from films to foreign documentaries. In most departments, including Birmingham and Surrey, teaching methods therefore aim to promote "student-centred learning". This means that they encourage you to be responsible for your own learning and for the organisation of your work, and to set high standards and goals, such as near-native competence in your target languages. The role of the teacher in this process is to encourage and support you, to guide your learning and to engage in an exchange of ideas with you. **"**

How would you show these skills in your personal statement?

Do most of your friends expect to go to university and do your parents want you to continue in full-time education?

Your friends and parents will not have to do the work you are asked to do at university. By all means listen to them but be yourself. You cannot just do what others want you to do. If your gut feeling is that you need time away from full-time education before applying, then take that time. Taking a gap year is one way of giving you this space to think. However, I would normally suggest that unless you are dead set on not going to university, you apply for a deferred place (you take a gap year before you start) rather than apply post-A level.

Are you clear about the career you want to pursue and do you expect to have to get a degree to start this career?

Some careers such as medicine, architecture, nursing and engineering require vocational degree qualifications. Your personal statement needs to show evidence of your commitment to these careers before you apply. Have you completed work experience and if so, what did you learn? Have you taken time to speak to practitioners or even worked for companies in that industry part time?

What reasons might you have for not going to university?

Think about what you might do if you do not go to university. Are you going for good reasons? If not, and you are not committed to a course, this will show in a personal statement that lacks clarity and personal enthusiasm.

Are you the first person in your immediate family to consider going to university?

The government is very keen, as are most universities, to recruit more students from currently under-represented backgrounds. Research suggests that students who meet these criteria are less likely to apply:

- Students whose family is from socio economic groups III to V (this means that your parents work in semi-skilled manual/non-manual jobs, unskilled jobs or are unemployed)
- People with disabilities
- Mature students – students who are over 23 years old
- People from certain ethnic minorities.

If you think you are a student from one or more of these backgrounds, you may qualify for additional support in preparing your application from university 'widening participation' officers. They often run taster courses, advice clinics and other incentives to encourage you to apply. If in doubt, ask to speak to an officer at one of the universities in which you are most interested.

Should students from these groups indicate this on their application form or personal statement?

This struck me as an important question to ask the admissions tutors who collaborated with this book. If there was an advantage to be had if you were considered a widening participation applicant, this ought to be made clear in your personal statement or academic reference.

The answers we received from the universities varied. Some were adamant that they did not look at the socio economic group at all. They simply accepted pupils based on academic potential regardless of their background.

Others did look at the school to see what success it had when admitting students and this may favour a borderline candidate. A good candidate from a school with little or no history of sending students to university would be given extra credit.

Others advise you to be explicit if you are from a group that meets the widening participation criteria. You should mention it if you are the first in your immediate family to attend university or that you are in a family that is economically disadvantaged. This is perhaps best done in the final paragraph of your personal statement and this is what I encourage my students to do. The school should also allude to this in their academic reference.

The following are direct quotes from a number of different university departments.

❝ The Institute of Archaeology very much supports the Widening Participation agenda, and has undertaken numerous activities to encourage applicants from a wide range of backgrounds, including taster days, masterclasses, and events in National Archaeology Week. As a discipline, archaeology has traditionally attracted a very broad spectrum of applicants, including a high proportion of adult learners. ❞
UNIVERSITY COLLEGE, LONDON

❝ We've always encouraged widening participation and invite a large proportion of people who apply to us to come to our auditions. It can be helpful to see an explanation that someone has not had the opportunities to take part in a range of acting roles simply because of their personal circumstances. This would not in any way debar from audition. ❞
LIVERPOOL INSTITUTE OF PERFORMING ARTS

❝ The University of Southampton's approach to widening participation is focused around encouraging, recruiting and supporting people who have the ability, enthusiasm and potential to succeed at university, but who come from groups that are currently under-represented in higher education and the University of Southampton itself. The University also offers bursary schemes to support its

widening participation agendas, meaning that one-third of its students receive a University of Southampton Bursary. We do not currently take into account in the admissions process whether or not a student has a family history of higher education, with the exception of the BM6 Medicine programme. **'**
UNIVERSITY OF SOUTHAMPTON

All admissions tutors recognised that some issues that the applicant may want to raise, that were pertinent to the application, may be too private for a public document. Such issues could be expressed in a letter sent direct to the admissions office of each university. Too few applicants disclose this sort of information and this is detrimental to them and their application. All letters sent would be considered in confidence. Such letters should be supported by medical opinion, social work reports or other third party agency testimonials, where such support is appropriate. (*You are advised not to mention anything in your personal statement that you would not want read by too many people – this is the beauty of the supplementary letter.*)

Note: these letters should not be sent until **after** the application has been sent to UCAS and the applicant has received the letter of confirmation from UCAS.

Do you have any special educational needs?
No university indicated that they were concerned about special educational needs (SEN) disclosures. Such students will not be prejudiced in any way and indeed they may find that extra support is available to support them when at university. There is no harm in mentioning in your personal statement that you have a particular SEN, particularly if you have overcome this and been successful.

What happens next?
The final stage of research before you start to write your statement considers the two most important questions:

- What should I study?
- Where should I study?

CHAPTER THREE

WHAT COURSE TO STUDY AND WHERE?

Before you start making an application and writing your personal statement, I want you to take some time to consider what it is you want to study and where? Many students just 'end up' at university without giving any serious thought to the nature of the course and location.

First, write down your answers to the following questions – you will refer to them again when you start to write your statement.

- List at least four reasons why it is important for you to go to university? (in order of importance to you).
- Have you a particular subject or course in mind?
- If your answer is yes, can you write down some the factors . . . that influence your choice? In particular, think about the skills or attributes you possess that support your interest.
- If your answer is no, can you at least isolate the skills you have that you want to enhance and develop at university. These might include literary, mechanical, design, mathematical, artistic or sporting skills. It is clearly worthwhile playing to your strengths.
- Have you a clear career path in mind? Will this career require any qualifications that you can gain at university or college?
- Do you want to live near your home or would you be willing to move a long way away? Is location an important factor in your decision-making?
- Do you have a university in mind as your first choice? If so, what reasons can you give that support this choice? Do you know that the course requirements meet your expectations and academic potential?
- What about the other choices? You can make up to five in total, unless you are applying to medical, dental or veterinary school where you can only apply for four.

WHAT TO STUDY?

You need to really know yourself and know the departments you hope to persuade to accept you. You must do your research and make it clear in the application and your personal statement that you have done this thoroughly. As you will see in the academic profiles, often admissions tutors refer to students applying with little understanding of the demands of the course. These applications and personal statements are more often than not consigned to the reject pile.

To research universities effectively, you can:

- Use the excellent UCAS website (www.ucas.ac.uk)
- Read books and websites (listed on pages 203–204)
- Read carefully the websites of the universities and take the chance to visit them.

You will live there and study there for three years, so it is foolish to commit without ever walking the streets of the town or peering into the libraries and halls of residence.

THE UCAS WEBSITE

The UCAS website (www.ucas.ac.uk) is an excellent site, full of useful advice. It has a comprehensive course search facility that allows you to access every course that is offered in the UK through the UCAS system. It allows you to compare courses and find out more about the nature of the courses.

Do use the course search facility as an initial sift. Look at the 'entry profiles' that have been compiled by all the universities. These give a good insight into what they are looking for in a good candidate.

STAMFORD TEST AND UCAS-ENDORSED CENTIGRADE

The Stamford Test is a short questionnaire that can help to match your interests and abilities to possible higher education subjects. Many students find this extremely helpful when trying to make up their minds.

The test is extremely easy to use and I recommend that all my students do the test as part of their research activity. To do it, you need to register with UCAS.

Another popular and UCAS-endorsed test is 'Centigrade' that is designed and promoted by Cambridge Occupational Analysts (COA). Centigrade goes into much more detail, matching a student's interests, current academic grades, preferred degree subjects and likely range of UCAS tariff points scores to direct them to up to eight course areas. Once you have answered the questionnaire, COA will send you a detailed bound report with well-matched selections. Centigrade can be completed online or using a paper questionnaire. The cost is £17 for a full colour printed personal report (approx 48 pages). For further information phone COA on 01362 688722 or go to www.coa.co.uk.

WHERE TO STUDY?

There will be many reasons why it is inappropriate or appropriate to apply to a particular university – these include academic grade expectation, cost of living, course content, proximity to home, graduate employment prospects and location (rural vs. urban; campus vs. non-campus.) All these factors need to be teased out **before** you start to write your statement.

My students often ask what the right university is for them. Here is my answer that I trust will help you compose your own. In short, the best university is the one that best suits **the individual student!**

It is the university that offers you:

- A course that is interesting
- A good quality of teaching
- A favourable geographical location
- A realistic and achievable conditional offer
- A good graduate employment record
- A range of excellent facilities, not least accommodation.

Choosing a course that is interesting and has good quality teaching

When doing your research, the following tips are useful:

- Check the research and teaching rating for the relevant course on the latest league tables. League tables are a good place to start, but do not reject those whose research rating is lower than 4.

Tables are useful, but need to be treated as starting points not ends in themselves.

- The premier league of the British university system include the Russell Group universities. They are the ones with the best research ratings overall, the best reputation with employers (normally) and highest kudos. Most commentators suggest that the following are in the 'Premier' league (not all in the Russell Group): Birmingham, Bristol, Cambridge, Cardiff, Durham, Edinburgh, Glasgow, Imperial, King's London, Leeds, Liverpool, LSE, Manchester, Newcastle, Nottingham, Oxford, Sheffield, Southampton, St Andrew's, Sussex, UCL, Warwick and York.

- The best course for **you** may not be at one of the so-called 'best' universities. You need to consider other factors, most notably employment prospects, course content and location.

- Look at some of the books available to help you such as Brian Heap's *Choosing your Degree Course and University.* He does a lot of the hard work for you, giving a brief summary of each institution and their courses. It is updated every two years and published by Trotman. It is not cheap, so look for it in a school, college or local library.

- Ask for your own copy of all the relevant prospectuses. You can order them via email by going to the university website. Online prospectuses are also first rate and are usually updated before each admissions cycle. They can often provide more up to date information than the expensive looking paper copies. They also provide details of open days and taster events. These 'taster' events are particularly useful when preparing the first part of your personal statement.

Further research opportunities

You will find many books, websites, magazines and prospectuses to help you make these two vital decisions. My favourites are in the Further Reading section.

However, I am now going to assume that you have done the reading, asked the questions and thought about your options. We shall now start to write your statement that will hopefully be part of your passport to the course that you crave!

FACTORS IN YOUR CHOICE

The right geographical location	Do you want to live away from home? There are personal development factors to be gained when living away from home and this can prove significant when seeking a job.
An offer that realistically you are going to achieve	You need to balance optimism with pragmatism. Ask yourself what you really expect to achieve and what evidence from past performance you can point to in your statement and academic reference to support this. There is no point applying for a course that you cannot reasonably expect to get into with your predictions or subject profile.
A good employment record for recent graduates	If you are clear about what you want to do after university, the subject must provide a suitable basis for that career.
A range of excellent facilities, including accommodation	The facilities offered by universities are similar: they will all have a library, a sports hall, and careers service. However, if you require a specialised facility, then this is a factor to consider. A climber is not advised to go to East Anglia if he or she wants access to mountains!

CHAPTER FOUR

YOUR PERSONAL STATEMENT: GETTING STARTED

Your personal statement is, I believe, the most important piece of writing that you will complete outside of the examination hall. For that reason alone, it is vital to take the time to get it right. Most universities in the UK do not have the resources to select via interview. Cambridge interviews almost all candidates whose applications are considered worthy of further exploration; Oxford do the same in some subjects but 'deselect' between 20% and 25% of applicants for some subjects. Other universities do interview, but they tend to be for highly competitive courses, vocational courses such as medicine, veterinary science or nursing. Artists and architecture applicants are often interviewed to examine their portfolio and drama and music students should expect an audition.

The application form is, therefore, the only medium that most students can use to sell themselves. Note my use of the word 'sell'. This is deliberate. The British are often reluctant to sell themselves well; they think that it is either boasting, evidence of an over-inflated ego or worse!

This is a mistake. You need to write in a way that is persuasive, emphasises your strengths, minimises your weaknesses and essentially 'sells' you (the applicant) to the reader (the admissions tutor). The admissions tutor is the 'gatekeeper' and if it is not engaging, undersells your achievements or is poorly constructed then the tutor will be less inclined towards to offering you a set of keys!

How do the universities use your statement?
The University of Leicester student support service suggests on its website that your personal statement gives you the opportunity to:

- Help the university find out about you and your suitability for the course they have to offer
- Present your goals, experiences and qualifications in the best possible light

- Demonstrate your writing ability
- Distinguish yourself from the other applicants.

Note: if a candidate is unfortunate enough not to achieve the grades of the offer, often the admissions team read the statement again if they are toying with taking an applicant anyway!

THE BASICS

Most UK students use the UCAS online system **Apply** (www.ucas.ac.uk/ students/apply/) to process their application. UCAS expects you to enter the personal statement directly into the application and limit the word count.

You cannot write more than 4,000 characters or 47 lines of text in a standard font. I recommend that you use font size 12 (Times New Roman). This is important as the page is reduced from A4 to A5, so smaller writing can make it illegible. You cannot use italics, bold or underline words, as these will not be transferred into the Apply package. Inexplicably, neither will accents such as é.

Don't waste your time on fancy formatting. Apply will not allow indented lines or coloured fonts. Apply does allow all the common punctuation marks and the following symbols:

! £ $ % ^ & * () @ # ~ ? – =
but **not**
€ © ∞

I also recommend disabling the 'auto format' feature in Microsoft Word as this can mean that dashes and quotation marks are removed from the submitted personal statement.

The Apply software does not have a spell-checking facility. You should write your statement using a word processing package. Once it has been *thoroughly* checked for spelling (make sure you have put UK spell check as your default!), punctuation and grammar, you can cut and paste it into Apply.

In my experience, many applicants leave the first draft of the statement until the very last moment, sometimes weeks or months after they have chosen their course. Teachers are busy, too, and although sixth-form UCAS tutors are usually experienced, leaving things to the last minute can lead to errors slipping through. This is more often than not the fault of the student, so start early and keep to school or college deadlines!

WHEN TO START

This is an easy question as the answer is succinct – early! By that I mean during your lower sixth-form year. I ask my students to write a draft in the gap between the end of their AS exams and the end of the summer term. This forces them to:

- Make some early decisions about what to study
- Look at themselves critically
- Begin the research that is vital to prevent poor choices in the long term
- Do something constructive rather than vegetate while waiting for the term to end!

It does mean that they return in the autumn with something to go on. The autumn term is very busy and anything that puts you ahead of the game is worthwhile. This is particularly true if you need to apply early – by 15th October, for places at Oxford, Cambridge, medical, veterinary or dental schools. If you want to apply for an Oxbridge choral or organ scholarship, you will need to get it done in the first week of September!

A good personal statement will probably take three weeks to write. So do not leave it till the last minute.

THE STRUCTURE OF YOUR STATEMENT

YOUR STATEMENT: QUESTIONS TO ASK YOURSELF		
First section	40%	Your choice of subject to study at university
Second section	35%	The subjects you are currently studying
Third section	25%	Your extracurricular interests and achievements

Your statement should answer these questions succinctly and in a style that is engaging and informative. You need to have evidence to support your claims, so think about what evidence you might provide.

First section: your choice of subject

- Why have you chosen to read the subject at university?
- What is the background to your interest in the subject?
- For how long have you had this interest?
- What particular areas of your studies appeal most and why?

These questions are particularly pertinent if you are applying for a vocational degree, such as medicine, nursing, law or physiotherapy.

Mention any relevant work experience, summer employment or voluntary work that supports your application. This is vital when applying for all medical-based courses where they will expect you to have arranged suitable work experience. For instance, you will not be interviewed for a physiotherapy course if you have not done at least two weeks work placement.

- Have you completed any relevant taster courses in preparation for your degree course such as Headstart, VETSIX or Medlink?
- Have you taken part in a NAGTY (National Academy for Gifted and Talented Youth) course?
- Have you spent any time on a residential course run by a university?
- What did you learn?
- How useful were the courses?

These are very good selling points that you must emphasise.

- What are your career aspirations?

Mention this if it is pertinent to the subject you wish to read.

Second section: the subjects you are currently studying

- What particular interests do you have within you current AS and A2 (or equivalent) courses?
- How have they helped you choose the course?

Mention all of your subjects and briefly explain which parts of the course you have found most interesting and why. However, where a subject is directly relevant to the subject you are hoping to read, greater bias must be given to your enjoyment and skills in that discipline.

■ What evidence of wider reading or experience beyond the syllabus can you produce, particularly within the subjects directly relevant to your chosen subject?

This is crucial and often grossly underestimated. Many applicants simply do not read anything beyond their textbooks. This is not a successful way to convince an admissions tutor that you deserve to spend three more years studying them to degree level! You should name books, articles or media events that have inspired or challenged you, and be able to explain why. Listing a series of books without evaluation of at least one main theme is mere namedropping. If you are likely to be called for interview, be prepared to discuss some of the references at length. In other words **do not lie**!

Third section: your extracurricular pursuits and skills

This section focuses particularly on your extracurricular pursuits (both in and out of school or college). You can also emphasise important skills you possess such as leadership, initiative and personal skills.

These final paragraphs should give evidence of these areas:

■ **Extracurricular subjects:** What subjects are you studying outside the curriculum?
■ **Other achievements:** These achievements should be substantive and show that you are both able and dedicated. High grades in music or drama exams, Duke of Edinburgh's Awards, combined cadet force (CCF) or Scout awards are all worthy examples.
■ **Leadership potential:** Give evidence of your leadership potential, how you were selected (elected?) and what you learned from leading your team.
■ **Inside school:** Have you held positions of significant responsibility, for example head boy or girl, house captain, official; chair of the

student council, debating society, enterprise teams, 2.5% interest rate challenge, or sports captain.

■ **Outside school:** Local political party work, charity work, church choir, uniformed organisation, young church leader, non-school sporting achievement.

■ **Other successes:** Details of significant other successes you have enjoyed – these may include community and charity work, for example, running the London Marathon, or anything else that sets you apart from the couch potatoes with their eyes glued to Sky or the latest PS3 game!

■ **Gap year:** Mention any gap year plans you have, accentuating the positive advantages of such a gap year for your future vocation. Most universities are happy to offer you a deferred place but Oxbridge tends not to encourage deferred applications for mathematicians and that is also true of other major universities. This is something to consider research and consider carefully before you fill in your UCAS form.

I have deliberately divided the statement into two large sections and one smaller section. Universities are places of academic study and research. Most admissions tutors are highly educated, committed (sometimes devoted) to their subject and keen to work with like-minded undergraduates.

They want to recruit students with other interests, too. However, being a good rugby player, musician and pool player will not cut much ice if your academic profile is weaker than the next applicant.

CHAPTER FIVE
HOW TO AVOID A POOR PERSONAL STATEMENT

These tips are all drawn from experience and as a result of direct advice from admissions tutors. You should read them together with the academic profiles on pages 61. They will give specific advice about different academic disciplines and are therefore well worth reading carefully.

- **Clarity:** Avoid waffle, generalisations and poor sentence construction. Be precise and concise. Say what you mean in a clear, uncluttered manner.
- **Tone:** Avoid humour – this is a professional document. Weak applicants misjudge the tone of the document they are writing.
- **Style:** Avoid 'text-speak', colloquial slang and language that may offend.
- **Length:** Use the full amount of space that you can. This is probably the most important document you have written outside of an exam hall in your life. If you cannot say enough about your passion for the subject and why you are an interesting person to teach to fill the full 47 lines, what does that say about you?
- **Enthusiasm:** Don't be dull – dry, uninspiring prose indicates a dry, uninspiring applicant. Appear very interested, enthusiastic and well read with an informed judgement about what the course is about.
- **Sell yourself:** Promote your achievements and potential.
- **Language:** Avoid poor spelling, grammar and punctuation. This is crucial if you want to be taken seriously in any application you make, be it to university or a job. If this is a personal weakness that you are aware of, ask someone else to proofread your statement. This is particularly relevant if you are an international student or if English is not your first

language. Applications without spelling mistakes have been known to receive offers; those with mistakes may be self-penalising.

- **Be yourself:** Don't try to be the 'ideal' applicant. They want to get to know you, not the person you are pretending to be. After all, if you kid them into taking you and then start the course, you may find that you are not cut out for it when you start. This is both demoralising and expensive if you subsequently leave.

- **Avoid plagiarism:** Do not copy anyone else's personal statement. You will read exemplary personal statements in this book, written by successful applicants. Learn from them and the advice given by the tutors who picked them. Please do not copy them – this gives a false impression to the tutor and is fraudulent. You are asked to sign that everything in the application is correct to your knowledge. Any lies or plagiarism uncovered will be treated seriously and may jeopardise your application. Most universities now employ tools to detect plagiarism among their own students.

UCAS studied 50,000 forms in 2007 and found that a large number of applicants cheated by copying material from websites offering advice on how to apply.

UCAS is employing a new system called 'Copycatch', which will compare every application submitted with thousands posted on websites and over a million submitted in previous years. If three sentences or more – 10% of your statement – appear to have been copied, the form will be passed to staff for further scrutiny. Be warned!

Before we start to construct your statement, here are some final thoughts for you to consider.

The aim of this guide is to provide you with information that is clear, current and supported by the universities. A successful personal statement and UCAS application as a whole is one that stand outs.

MORE QUESTIONS TO ASK

These questions are more focused on the drafting stage. You need to write your answers down so that you can look at them again, together with the other notes you have already made.

What subject/subjects do you want to study at university? List the reasons you are drawn to this subject.

This is one of the key elements of any successful personal statement. You need to have a pithy and well-written statement of why you want to study your chosen subject with some supporting evidence that will back up your claims.

Who or what has influenced you the most to study your subject?

For example, is there something that's triggered your interest in the subject – did you go to a lecture or have a really good teacher? Or if you've just read a book, mention that. But don't make it up. If you have not had any particular 'eureka' moment, and it is just a subject that you've loved at school, then say so.

What wider reading have you done to support this application?

Do not just mention the books you have had to read in the A level course! What magazines, newspapers and internet sites do you read or visit to extend your knowledge?

Have you attended taster courses or undertaken work experience? If appropriate list the plays, films or TV programmes you have seen and say how they have influenced you.

This evidence should be presented clearly in the opening paragraph of your personal statement.

(Continued)

What research have you undertaken that has led you to this degree choice?	I just want to be sure that you have done the research necessary to make this decision. Do you know the course content well and does this meet your own skills, interests and aspirations?
What subjects have you studied so far that supports this application? Do you require any particular subject at A level (or equivalent) to be accepted?	This is a vital part of a successful personal statement. Please do not fall into the trap of applying for a course that you cannot get into to because you lack the minimum academic credentials. Many admissions tutors I spoke to complained about this weak and lazy approach that was often exposed in the personal statement.
Can you list the skills that you have developed in each course you are studying (or have studied) that support your application?	These may be analytical, mathematical, problem solving, written, oral or simply subject specific. For instance, the study of maths may have taught you analytical skills, design spatial awareness or English the ability to read and write quickly and persuasively under pressure. This is a key component of the second section of a good personal statement.
What coursework projects or extended pieces of work have you been asked to do or completed as part of your course (if applicable)? What skills have you developed or do you expect to develop?	Universities are keen to hear about skills that you may have already developed that are linked to university teaching and assessment styles, particularly independent learning, research and extended essays.

What are your future intentions and goals? (after school and university)	This is relevant information to include in the final paragraph. If you are unsure, do not worry, as this is nice to know information but by no means critical. You may want to mention any gap year plans but only if they will enable you to be a more proficient or able student as a result. For instance, foreign travel to a country whose language you hope to study.
What extracurricular accomplishments do you wish to draw to the attention of the admission tutors and why?	These are important to mention in the final section of your statement. Concentrate on a few significant achievements, particularly if they involve leadership roles, personal initiative, team building skills or the attainment of recognised qualifications.

SUMMARY

You will now have answered many questions that are all relevant to your personal statement. You now need to look again at the notes you have made of your answers.

At this stage try to draw the notes into three groups that suit the three distinct sections of the personal statement. To remind you – the first stage is broadly speaking a clear explanation of why you want to study that course together with evidence to support this interest. The second section is a summary of the skills and attributes that you have acquired through the study of your A levels or their equivalents, with special emphasis on the skills that are most relevant. The final section is a summary of your extra curricular pursuits, placing particular emphasis on the activities that emphasise your leadership potential or personal initiative.

Look again at the advice given in Chapter four for further help. Once done, you can start the first section of your statement.

CHAPTER SIX
THE FIRST SECTION: YOUR CHOICE OF SUBJECT

First impressions really do count. Look at the successful personal statements provided by universities later in this book. Giving your personal statement a strong opening will engage the reader's attention from the outset. Common mistakes include the use of clichéd and overused sentences in the introduction. For example, you should avoid starting your sentence with the following:

'I have always wanted to study . . .'

as this is patently not the case; or

'My passion has always been for . . .'

which is a similarly unlikely claim for any 18-year-old to make! You should instead imply an interest in your chosen course. You need to quickly show the admissions tutor that you have a genuine interest, and this requires the use of specific examples.

Look back at your answers to the questions in Chapter Five – what examples can you give?

Perhaps it is the books that you have read beyond the syllabus, the lecture you attended in your free time, the taster course you paid to attend in the holidays or the work experience placement you have either completed or arranged.

You could refer to a leader in the field of your interest that has inspired you – for instance a philosophy and politics applicant could write about Plato's *Republic* and its views on the structure of democracy and justice.

You may refer directly to an event or person in your life that has inspired you – for instance a student of mine recently wrote about her interest in medicine being linked to the fact that she has lived with a genetic disease. Her personal investigation into this illness – its aetiology and likely development – plus repeated exposure to medical professionals was the genesis of her desire to study medicine.

You will also need to draw attention to any work experience that is relevant and most importantly what you learnt while undertaking this experience.

WORK EXPERIENCE

It is vital to mention relevant work experience in the opening half of the personal statement if the course requires it. Admissions tutors ask applicants to get relevant experience for two main reasons:

- **To demonstrate commitment to your career choice:** Just enjoying *Holby City* does not justify a strong desire to work as a doctor. A committed applicant to medicine must demonstrate a commitment to the community, which could mean working as a hospital porter during the holidays, attending a hospice as a helper over six months, spending at least one day in a GP's surgery or taking the time to arrange a meeting with a consultant.
- **So that they can be sure you are going into this career path with your eyes open:** You've seen the reality of the job, warts and all, and it hasn't put you off. A potential applicant to teacher training needs to be aware that pupils are not always well-behaved and that teaching involves a great deal of time-consuming administration. They learn this by sitting in with a primary class and talking to teachers at their local senior school. In my experience, schools are nearly always willing to offer a potential undergraduate the opportunity to do this if they write well in advance.

The most common courses that expect work experience are:

Medicine: They would expect at least two discrete work experience placements. Many hospitals now do not offer ward-based work experience to those under 18. Try your local hospital's human resources department but do not be surprised by a refusal. This is where lateral thinking comes in: care homes and hospices are also medical settings, and helping out for, say, half a day each week over a long period can be even more beneficial than just two days on a hospital ward. You are also quite likely to be able to arrange a visit to your local GP to have lunch with a doctor to discuss his or her career and recent issues in the NHS that may come up in an interview. A well-crafted letter to your own GP can pay dividends. Mentoring younger pupils in your own school can help your interpersonal skills, and work with disabled teenagers promotes empathy.

Dentistry: My experience is that dental surgeries are generally happy to have a well-chosen potential dentist in their surgery for a few days. They might expect you to cover in reception, observe some routine procedures, talk to the hygienist and in return help out with the filling! I recommend contacting your own dentist, preferably including a reference from your school or college testifying to your genuine interest and academic potential.

Nursing and midwifery: Queen Mary's, University of London (QMUL) suggest that care homes and hospices are excellent settings in which students can find out if they are really suited to this type of work. For midwifery, applicants should contact their local hospital's midwifery service manager to arrange experience in the maternity unit – most universities will require a minimum of one day's experience, if nothing else, so that students can learn that being a midwife is not about babies! It's actually about looking after the mothers.

Physiotherapy: Similarly the QMUL website says that physiotherapy is probably one of the most competitive courses a student can apply for, so getting work experience is essential. Most jobs are in the NHS, so experience in this setting should be the student's main priority, even if they are aiming to work in sport (a growing, but still very small, area of physiotherapy work). It is sometimes possible to get a paid (rarely) or voluntary physiotherapy assistant post in an NHS hospital; failing that, shadowing a chartered physiotherapist is the next best thing.

Veterinary science: There are only six vet schools in the UK and competition to get in is fierce, although the myth that you need all A*s at GCSE needs exploding! Potential applicants need to spend time with both small and large animals and this may be problematic if you live in an urban environment.

However, most vet surgeries are used to written requests for help, so start there. Think laterally – you may live near a children's farm; they look after animals and you could volunteer to work there. One successful student that I knew did this at a local children's farm from the age of 14. She is now a successful vet in London. If you own a pony or horse, the stables will have qualified professionals on hand to advise.

Teaching: Most degree courses that integrate Qualified Teacher Status (QTS) will interview and expect some relevant work experience. Evidence that you have worked with children elsewhere is also important – so get involved with local scout groups, youth clubs or programmes working with children in the holidays such as the Barracuda organisation. You will need to undertake an enhanced disclosure test to work with children.

Note: all of the above will expect you to undertake an enhanced disclosure test or Criminal Records Bureau Check (CRB) and, in the case of medicine, be inoculated against certain diseases (especially Hepatitis B) before you start the course.

Here are some examples of excellent opening paragraphs from real personal statements that were all successful in gaining offers at Oxford, Cambridge or other leading universities.

THE HISTORY APPLICANT

E. H. Carr called History 'an unending dialogue between the present and the past', a concept that has always fascinated me. Each age will see something different in the past as being 'significant'. History tells us not only about the nature of the past, but about the nature of the age in which History is written. For example, the way current historians interpret the Crusades is informed by the present situation in the Middle East but also needs to take into account the views of historians contemporary to those cataclysmic events. The concept of a 'clash of civilisations' needs to be tested in both the present and in the past.

THE ENGLISH APPLICANT

The study of English Literature has undoubtedly shaped the way I think. Philosophical deliberation has been a necessity in the reading of both Paradise Lost and Hamlet, for example, with Milton's attempts to 'justify the ways of God to men' being pertinent to Hamlet's lamentation of the human condition and what he perceives to be the sheer inevitability of suffering through life. The exploration of the historical contexts behind these two works has been equally absorbing, with the similarities between the God of Paradise Lost, and the king condemned by Milton, lending a particularly revealing insight to Milton's own disposition. Indeed, through learning English, I have encountered a wide range of disciplines, and it is the extreme diversity offered by the subject that makes it so wonderful and informative for me; rigorous analytical thought is developed through practical criticism, while the flexibility and creativity of writing is cultivated through essay and prose composition.

THE ARCHAEOLOGY AND ANTHROPOLOGY APPLICANT

Having spent the first 13 years of my life in Kenya, it was always going to be a culture shock when I moved to England four years ago. My time in both countries has given me a better perspective on the globe on which we live. From a young age I was fascinated by the human race. Through visits to Samburu and Maasai settlements and day-to-day living in Nairobi, I began to realise the great diversity within human culture, further revealed by trips to Kenya's Islamic coast and then by a move to England. Here I experienced a very different outlook and a very different way of life, captured well in Watching the English by Kate Fox. My own life has triggered a need to understand more about the reasons for these differences. I hunger to learn about 'the self' while studying 'the other', to know who we are and how we got where we are. Anthropology is the obvious route to this knowledge.

THE MODERN LANGUAGES APPLICANT

To me, language in its essence represents a key to another culture, opening the door to a world of new experiences. Since childhood I have been amazed by the vast difference in thinking and lifestyle on opposite sides of the Channel. Visiting France annually with my family, such contrasts have fascinated me, and in studying the French language I have attempted to become more than just an observer, but rather a participant and appreciator. The wealth of cultural thrills that this has imparted is my greatest motivation in taking my study of French to university level, as well as expanding the possibility of such opportunities in the study of Spanish.

SUMMARY

Draft this first section carefully using a word processor. Make sure that you ask advice from a teacher or tutor and that it is read by at least two people who can check it for quality and possible error. Do not worry too much at this stage about length. It is easier to précis a long well-written piece then to pad it out. You will in the end need to cut it down to meet the length requirements but this can wait until later.

CHAPTER SEVEN

THE SECOND SECTION: THE SUBJECTS YOU ARE CURRENTLY STUDYING

 our personal statement must proceed in a logical succession from one thought to the next. The body of your personal statement should lead in a convincing way from the introduction to conclusion.

The second section should focus on the skills you have already gained while at school or college. When talking about your educational background, do not just mention what is clear from the rest of your application. They can read how many GCSEs you got elsewhere.

The primary focus should be on any A level courses that are directly relevant to your choice of degree. The historian should talk about his or her History A level first and at greatest length. Focus on what you have learned and what skills you have honed.

When you introduce your other AS or A level subjects, it is wise to draw attention to the ways in which your other subjects have complemented your skills and learning in the principal subject.

- Talk first and foremost about the subjects that you are currently or recently finished studying that are directly relevant to your choice of degree. How have they helped you choose the course?
- Do not repeat what an admissions tutor can read elsewhere – telling them how many GCSEs you have got is irrelevant.
- Do mention, however, if you have any very high marks in AS or GCSE papers – this sets you apart from the rest. By this I mean that you may have obtained 100% in one paper or full marks in your extended or project work.
- Mention any coursework or extended work that you have completed that suggest that you are capable of independent learning. This is an important facet of university teaching and learning.

- Mention the other subjects that may not be directly relevant, but have enabled you to gain useful skills.
- Quote books, magazines, websites or courses that you may have read or attended. However, do not lie as this can be exposed at a later date and lead to rejection.

A good example of this can be found in these extracts from real personal statements.

THE MODERN LANGUAGES APPLICANT

While at school I have gained eight academic prizes, including three for French and two for Latin. My study of Latin has been particularly useful for setting up a framework within which to learn languages, as well as for its rich history and literature. In English, I have nurtured a love for literature and developed analytical and evaluative skills. Studying History at AS helped me come to a greater understanding of the foundations of our European culture, as well as similarly furthering analytical and evaluative technique.

THE MEDICAL APPLICANT

Biology has made me appreciate the complexity of life processes like respiration and photosynthesis. I find the biochemistry part of these processes, such as glycolysis, intriguing as it covers ideas that I have learnt from chemistry as well. Finally in philosophy I have been introduced to important ideas about how the mind and body are connected, as well as looking at key ethical dilemmas related to medicine, including euthanasia and abortion. I am also taking critical thinking as an extra AS level in my spare time. This is teaching me how to analyse data and arguments, which will be important in making impartial decisions in a clinical setting.

CHAPTER EIGHT

THE THIRD SECTION: YOUR EXTRACURRICULAR INTERESTS AND ACHIEVEMENTS

This is the final paragraph and should focus on your extracurricular pursuits. Although your academic potential is top of their minds, admissions tutors do want to recruit students who will bring other skills to the department and university as a whole. They are looking for someone who is academically motivated but not a couch potato.

You need in this section to attempt to show some distinct skills or personality traits. Here are the key skills that admissions tutors tell us they look for:

- Persistence
- Independence
- Self-motivation
- Leadership
- Maturity.

Think now about what you do outside the classroom. What are your primary extracurricular pursuits? How have these pursuits helped you develop the skills that admissions tutors are looking for?

Add a concluding sentence or two. This will tie everything together. Integrate all the information gathered in the above paragraphs and finish on two positive sentences. The closing sentence must be powerful and succinct.

- Emphasise personal attributes that might include organisational skills, punctuality, sensitivity, responsibility, initiative, efficiency, communication and empathy. Where you mention one of these, give an example of what you have done to expose and develop this attribute.
- Mention any subjects that you are studying outside the formal curriculum, particularly if they are academic in their focus or lead to nationally recognised qualifications.

- Mention the extracurricular activities that you have undertaken. Don't just write a list. Concentrate on two or three activities that emphasise your personal qualities, such as leadership skills, initiative, sporting success or debating skills. The Duke of Edinburgh's Awards, Young Enterprise Scheme and combined cadet force (CCF) or Scouts are all particularly good examples.
- Emphasise any roles that you have held that were significant – particularly if you were elected or appointed by a senior teacher. For example, prefect status, captaincy of a sports team or elected head of an activity.
- Mention career plans or gap year plans – make sure that your gap year plans accentuate the positive advantages of such a gap year for your future vocation or university career.

Here are some examples of extracts from good final paragraphs that proved to be successful.

THE MEDICAL APPLICANT

For three years I have been a member of a storytelling group that travels across the country performing in events and festivals. Having to capture the imagination of an audience with only your voice and face has made me a confident and articulate person, which is highly important for a doctor who has to communicate with patients. My leadership skills were demonstrated at my comprehensive school as a prefect and a student council member. These taught me to be strict, reliable and fair.

THE HISTORY APPLICANT

I have taught myself GCSE Chinese, captained our successful school chess team for several years and completed the Silver Duke of Edinburgh's Award. I also have an active interest in politics and served as editor of our school political journal for a year. Debating is a particular passion of mine, and I will represent my school this coming year in the MACE competition.

THE GEOGRAPHY APPLICANT

Travel constitutes for me a real excitement, whether through school trips to the volcanoes and glaciers of Iceland and the eroded coast of Malta with its hugely exciting opportunities for scuba diving, or on journeys with the National Children's Orchestra to the Czech Republic and the County Youth Orchestra to Cyprus. Such travel has given me much food for thought on both economic and physical issues that impinge on globalisation. I have recently accepted an invitation to travel to Australia as a gap year student, mainly to teach hockey and other sports, an opportunity that would not only enhance my knowledge of geography, but also improve my leadership skills.

Another popular ending is one where you opt for a little self-promotion:

Overall I believe I have the necessary (academic/intellectual) ability, motivation and stamina to cope successfully with the demands of this subject and look forward to hearing from you in due course.

WIDENING PARTICIPATION

In Chapter Two I talked about the widening participation agenda to which all mainstream universities have signed up. Essentially, the aim is to encourage applications from students who are from social groups that are under-represented in UK universities. These include:

- Students from schools with a poor record of sending students to university
- Students from families whose parents are in semi- or unskilled employment
- Students who are the first in their family to attend university
- Mature students
- Students from certain ethnic backgrounds.

I advise you to allude to this, if it applies to you, in the final section of your statement. It is not clear to what extent it will influence admissions tutors. However, it can do no harm at all and at best may help persuade a tutor to take you if the decision is split.

A possible ending is reproduced here from an actual statement that helped win a place at medical school.

To study medicine is a dream that I have had since a small child, a dream that I am close to realising regardless of the fact that I have not enjoyed the benefits of an education in a school with greater experience of sending students to medical school. If successful I will be the first in my family to attend university and this is an opportunity that if offered I know that I would grasp and not let your faith in me down.

CHAPTER NINE
THE FINAL POLISH

 great personal statement is a work of art, not a hastily written paragraph or two. It takes time to research, plan, draft and then re-draft. Do not be afraid to redraft many times.

Use the three drafts that you have begun and if you have not already done so, word process your handwritten thoughts and begin the final drafting process.

The total length of the statement is 4,000 characters or 47 lines of text In a standard font. This is important, as the page is reduced from A4 to A5, so smaller writing can make it illegible.

You need to consider the following when you redraft.

- **SPAG** (Spelling, Punctuation and Grammar): Do not be guilty of poor SPAG. If you are, the impression you give is poor. As I intimated earlier, ask someone who is a competent proofreader to check this carefully.
- **Present yourself in the best possible light:** Make sure that your statement presents your goals, experiences and qualifications in the best possible light as well as demonstrating your writing ability. Have you mentioned the books you have read beyond the demands of the syllabus? Have you presented your work experience in the best possible light?
- **Get rid of any repetition or wasted words:** Do not say what is already apparent elsewhere in the application.
- **Avoid waffle, generalisations and poor sentence construction:** Be precise and concise. Say what you mean in a clear, uncluttered manner.
- **Avoid passive writing:** Rewrite sentences that use the phrase 'has been' or 'was'. These are words that are good to cull if you need to précis something that is too long.

Avoid the word 'I' as far as possible: Save the word I for when you need to write a short sentence that is full of emphasis such as 'I am a hard working, conscientious and ambitious student'.

Length: most of my students find the hardest part of the statement writing process lies in the careful précising that is necessary when it is 50 characters too long. This is a skill that requires time and effort. If you are really struggling, ask for advice from a teacher or fellow student who you know to be a good writer.

Be yourself, not the 'ideal' applicant: They want to get to know **you**, not the person you are pretending to be. You will spend three years studying that subject. Be sure that it is what you want, that you sell yourself well but fairly and that when you pass the exams in August and win that place you know that it is the right place for you.

Good luck!

CHAPTER TEN

CUKAS: HOW TO APPLY TO MUSIC CONSERVATOIRES

CUKAS is the online application process that is similar to UCAS and it is found at www.cukas.ac.uk. CUKAS is UCAS-owned and the service is designed to provide the facilities to research on and apply for practice-based music courses at the following UK conservatoires:

- Birmingham Conservatoire   www.conservatoire.uce.ac.uk
- Leeds College of Music   www.lcm.ac.uk
- Royal College of Music   www.rcm.ac.uk
- Royal Northern College of Music   www.rncm.ac.uk
- Royal Scottish Academy of Music   www.rsamd.ac.uk
  and Drama
- Royal Welsh College of Music   www.rwcmd.ac.uk
  and Drama
- Trinity College of Music   www.tcm.ac.uk

It offers a potential applicant a range of research tools and an online application form.

Note: not all UK conservatoires use CUKAS at the moment. Currently the Royal Academy of Music (www.ram.ac.uk) and the Guildhall School of Music and Drama (www.gsmd.ac.uk) do not use CUKAS and have their own application form and audition process. Please contact them direct via the internet or telephone to obtain the latest prospectus and application form.

This chapter will provide you with a sound understanding of why students apply to a conservatoire, how to apply online (including what to include in the personal statement) and what to expect at audition.

Why study at a conservatoire?

Conservatoire education is suitable for any talented musician who is particularly interested in performance, conducting or composition. They teach to a professional standard, combining practical and academic study in an environment that is steeped in musical history. Many of the teachers are leaders in their field and the UK is fortunate to have some of the finest conservatoires in Europe. Study in a conservatoire environment enables excellent networking and developmental opportunities for all musicians regardless of their specialism or musical direction.

Conservatoire students have the opportunity to conduct, perform or have their music performed on numerous occasions. Many of the performances are public and the students often find it is possible to earn money while at college playing at private parties and other functions. The range of music teaching available is vast including jazz, orchestral, operatic, musical theatre and choral.

Students study for three- or four-year undergraduate degrees (BA and BMus) as well as postgraduate programmes such as MMus and PgDip.

What are the entry standards?

As you can imagine, competition for places is high. Your traditional academic standards play 'second fiddle' to your performance standard. Each conservatoire has its own academic and performance demands. However, I will use information provided by the Royal College of Music (RCM) to provide you with an idea of demands likely to be placed on you and any other applicant. Most of this information is pertinent to all applicants but you are advised to look carefully at the prospectuses of the others.

The RCM currently has the following minimum entry requirements for the BMus (Hon).

- A level Music at grade C or above (most students achieve grade A or B), and either
- A second A level at grade E or above, or
- Two AS levels both at grade C or above (not including Music).

Music Technology is not accepted as a substitute for A level Music, but can be your second A level or one of your AS levels.

If you are not taking A level Music, but still wish to apply to the Royal College of Music, you may still be considered if you can demonstrate an appropriate level of musical knowledge and literacy. You may be tested/interviewed at audition to ascertain this.

Alternative entrance qualifications which are accepted instead of A levels are:

- Three Scottish Certificate of Education (SCE) Higher Grade passes, one of which should be in Music
- Advanced general national vocational qualifications (GNVQs)
- BTEC qualifications
- European or International Baccalaureate or other equivalent international qualifications.

What about auditions?

The Royal College has the following audition format:

- Auditions/interviews at the RCM are approximately 15–20 minutes long
- For some instruments and for voice you may be asked to perform at a second audition on the same day
- For set pieces see the Audition Pieces section of the online prospectus – www.rcm.ac.uk/Studying/How+to+Apply/Audition+ Pieces
- Technical work (for example, scales and arpeggios) may be required of some instrumentalists
- Sightreading may be required of all performers
- An accompanist can be provided by the RCM if required, but you are strongly advised to bring your own accompanist, with whom you will have worked in preparation for the audition.

Please note, each institution has its own audition procedure. Please research this information carefully.

When can I apply to CUKAS?

You can start an application in the July prior to attending the college the following year.

How many conservatoires can I apply to?

Up to six in one application cycle.

What costs are involved?

The cost of the application is similar to UCAS, £15. In addition you will be asked to pay audition fees. These vary from institution to institution.

Can I apply to CUKAS and UCAS in the same year?

Yes. Indeed, you are encouraged to do so as competition is so fierce that you need options to fall back on. You can apply to read music at university but there is nothing stopping you applying for something entirely different and then making up your mind at a later date. Keep you options open!

What should I include in a personal statement?

The advice is broadly similar to UCAS personal statements, except conservatoires are far more interested in your musical skills. The following points should be emphasised: Why you have chosen the courses you have listed. Unlike UCAS applications, each conservatoire will know where else you have to applied. Bear that in mind. You should mention:

- What local, national or international orchestras, choirs or chamber groups you are currently performing in, for instance National Youth Orchestra, National Youth Choir or European Union Youth Choir
- Your experience in composition and conducting
- The music and composers who have inspired you so far
- Any masterclasses you have attended, whether you have been involved in junior training programmes and any other gifted and talented initiatives
- What your career plans are, post application (if known)
- Any non-accredited skills and achievements that you have gained through such activities as Duke of Edinburgh's Awards, Young Enterprise or ASDAN (Award Scheme Development and Accreditation Network awards)
- Your sports, social or leisure interests
- Your gap year plans, if appropriate. You can apply for a deferred place.

As with all personal statements heed this basic advice:

- Make your interest in the subject evident in the opening few paragraphs with clear evidence supporting this from your study so far. You are writing for a tutor who shares this passion and wants to teach students with a genuine love for the subject. This may not always be possible, but whether it is or not, it is vital that the reader believes that you have thought about this application carefully and have good reasons to believe that you will thrive at that institution and department.
- Avoid spelling, punctuation and grammar errors. Get your statement proofread by someone who is competent to do so.
- Take advice where possible from a teacher who knows about the subject that you are hoping to apply for.
- Avoid plagiarism or lies.
- Emphasise your current skills and attributes, both academic and non-academic, in a positive and emphatic manner.
- Treat it as a very important piece of prose that deserves your best efforts – take your time to get it right and when it is, be proud of it and ready to defend what it says if your are called to interview.

How to fill in the application form

The form is completed online and in many ways it resembles the UCAS Apply system. The CUKAS site provides comprehensive advice and you should refer to www.cukas.ac.uk for more details. There are strict deadlines, so start as soon as possible and certainly start to prepare audition pieces with your music teacher/s.

PART TWO

ACADEMIC PROFILES

AMERICAN STUDIES

This academic profile was written using information provided by an admissions tutor from Swansea University. The information in this profile is useful to all applicants, but please be aware that some of the advice is pertinent to that department in particular.

SUBJECT OVERVIEW

As the last global superpower, the USA has an immediate and continuing impact on all our lives. It influences our culture, our economy, and our political outlook. Its foreign policy affects our future. To know and understand the nature of America, its art, culture, historical and political traditions, is to appreciate more fully the real forces driving the 21st century.

American studies is for students with a broad-based interest in American life and American culture, especially for those with a particular interest in American history, literature, politics, film or popular culture. It is also for students who would relish the opportunity to try out many different approaches (from film analysis to exploring the American landscape), develop new skills (such as decoding advertisements or studying historical documents) and explore many disciplines, which can also include art, music, communications and sociology alongside the core components of history, literature and politics and film. American studies can also be for those who would like to experience American life first-hand, with the opportunities to study four-year degrees at a number of higher education institutions and spend a whole year studying, travelling and exploring the USA. Students who choose a three-year degree are likely to have the experience of being taught by professors from the USA and could have the option of spending a semester studying in the USA depending on the course.

WHAT SKILLS OR ATTRIBUTES DO ADMISSIONS TUTORS LOOK FOR IN A GOOD APPLICANT?

American studies does not assume any prior study of American culture, but does assume that prospective students are interested in current affairs, are willing to engage with all aspects of American culture from gangsta rap to Hollywood blockbusters to *The Great Gatsby*, and are flexible and open-minded enough to cope with a wide range of teaching styles, methodological approaches and source material – whether presidential speeches, classic American novels or letters and memoirs from the American Civil War. Although most prospective students will have studied English, history, media or politics at A level, the nature of American studies is such that most departments will be more than willing to look at any candidate who possesses a real drive and enthusiastic commitment to studying the USA. Grade requirements vary, but on average you could expect to be asked to gain between ABB and BBC (or equivalent).

WHAT DOES A GOOD PERSONAL STATEMENT LOOK LIKE?

The most important thing to demonstrate when applying to American studies is a broad commitment to studying all aspects of American life and letters. Be as specific as you can – talk about American films you have enjoyed, American writers you are interested in, cover which aspects of American history (there's more of it than you might think!) especially excites you. You should also signal that you are aware of, and actively engaged with, contemporary issues – whether the Presidential election, events in Iraq, or all sorts of other global issues. American studies is a 'transnational' discipline, in that it also explores the impact of American policies and products on the rest of the world – thus you could also talk about issues of globalisation, foreign policy, or the relationship between America and the UK. Stress your flexibility and willingness to try new things – American studies requires a great deal of energy and adaptability as it covers so many different areas. If you have been to the US talk about your experience – even if it was only a family trip to Orlando, you can still touch upon what aspects of America you found familiar and any parts of American life which felt to you to be strangely 'foreign'. Talk about your interests and activities in a passionate and committed manner – we are looking for well-rounded individuals with a keen interest in a wide variety of fields.

Example of a good statement

> America is the most powerful and influential country in the world, as the phrase 'When America sneezes we all catch a cold' suggests.

✓ A good opening quote, and a clear understanding of the importance of the topic).

> I found studying Martin Luther King and civil rights at A level very interesting as well as America and the Vietnam War.

✓ Specific examples really add critical weight to the statement and give an indication of the areas that the candidate is already interested in.

> I have developed a further interest after visiting family in Arizona and experiencing first-hand the culture of America.

✓ While first-hand knowledge of America is not necessary, it does provide a basis for why the candidate might want to learn more.

> I want to read American Studies because I believe I will find it both interesting and fascinating.

✓ Enthusiasm and energy are key factors.

> I am interested in studying how the global superpower influences the culture, economy and political outlook in my daily life, United Kingdom, and the rest of the world.

✓ Suggests an awareness of, and interest in, global events and current affairs.

> I also feel it will further the skills and knowledge that I have already started building on in A levels. Not only have I learnt about America and some of its stages in history through college, but also due to my enjoyment of reading, I have read about it in books such as 'Little Women' and 'The Big Sleep'.

✓ The candidate covers both history and literature and strengthens their application by including specific titles and examples. A love of reading is very, very important!

> The subjects I have chosen for A levels are English Language, Sociology and History. These subjects have helped to provide skills such as time organisation and structured writing.

✓ Shows a clear understanding of the study skills required.

> They have also provided me with different ways in which to see the world, sociology showing the structure of society and the way people can act. In studying America it will be interesting to see the culture and society of another country and how it can change and develop. This will enable me to expand my views by challenging preconceived ideas to see whether they are right or wrong.

✓ The candidate understands that university education is about acquiring the skills to argue, discuss and debate.

> I have found studying History to be stimulating and challenging and it has helped me learn how to construct my ideas and arguments through assignments and essays. This has also helped me to develop analytical and evaluating skills which will be a great asset when studying American Studies. I'm looking forward to developing a greater depth of understanding of the world's largest superpower.

✓ A confident, well-written and critically focused conclusion.

This is an example of a very good personal statement. The candidate sets forward their reasons for undertaking the course, and demonstrates a real sense of commitment and academic drive. They also provide a number of specific examples of areas of American culture they have already found to be stimulating and provocative, choosing these from the central areas of both history (Vietnam, civil rights) and literature (*Little Women* and *The Big Sleep*). The candidate suggests in a clear and intelligent manner how the analytical skills they have already acquired will be of enormous relevance to their chosen degree scheme. They also demonstrate a lucid understanding of what the subject is, and the degree to which it matches their own interests and enthusiasms. The stress on the relationship between the USA and the UK, and indeed, America and the rest of the world also suggests an awareness of global issues and the importance of studying the basis and nature of American power and influence.

Example of a poor personal statement

> The current judicial system is far from perfect, but being able to change the views of people and help in the struggle for equality is very important to me.

✗ This seems both very vague and not really relevant to American studies – has the student applied to the right degree scheme?

> I feel that this is the perfect time to study with my good educational background and combination of business and General Studies.

✗ How does this relate to American studies? The candidate doesn't seem to be aware of the different elements that make up the scheme.

> Although I took my A levels in August 2006, I never thought about university, as I didn't think it was for me. However after nearly two years working for a telematic company I have become disillusioned in the workplace and can't imagine doing this line of work for the rest of my life, as I would like to make a difference, This is where applying for university comes in and gaining a degree as I strive for excellence.

✗ This seems very negative, as if the candidate is simply looking to escape the mundane nature of their current employment. Where is the commitment, the energy, or the imaginative enthusiasm? It is also a very badly constructed sentence.

> I am an independent, responsible and confident person who strives for perfection.

✗ Too vague – we need specific examples here.

> I can communicate with others who may find it difficult to do so, I can work independently and in a group, I can carry out tasks with minimum of help.

✗ The candidate needs to stress their critical and analytical skills rather than specifically work-related ones.

> My hobbies include playing football, Tennis, and anything sports-related. As I love challenging myself and trying to become the best I possibly can in whatever activity I am pursuing.

✗ The second sentence isn't a sentence – this gives the impression that the candidate is slipshod and puts very little effort into what they do.

This candidate makes no mention of American studies whatsoever; rather the distinct suspicion is that the candidate, unsure of where to go next, has applied to a wide range of courses (presumably including law or criminology) and has simply written a general and very sloppy personal statement. They fail to demonstrate any awareness of the degree scheme to which they are notionally applying, and the statement is particularly lacking in any concrete examples of why they would want to undertake American studies, or which aspects of the course (for example, film or history) they would find most interesting. The general tone is negative and unfocused; it feels as if the candidate is trapped in a dead-end job and will do anything to get out. Finally, as an individual who states that they strive for excellence, there are far too many errors in the piece – this gives the impression that the statement was cobbled together with very little thought or forward planning.

TOP TIPS FOR A GOOD PERSONAL STATEMENT

1 Be enthusiastic: You can do anything with your life right now – what drives you to choose American studies? Make this clear in your statement

2 Be relevant: Geal your reference to specific aspects of politics, literature, history or film

3 Name names: who are your favourite writers or film-makers, what history books have you read (and by whom?)

4 Assert your individuality: American studies allows you to mould the degree scheme around your own interests and ideas, so say what these are!

5 Be aware: of the news, of global events, of the economic and cultural forces that are all around us

6 Be specific: While joint honours students will want to discuss both aspects of their degree, it is important that you stress why you're *specifically* interested in American studies.

THINGS TO AVOID

1 Writing your application as if you simply want to visit the USA as a tourist! American studies is a challenging and academically rigorous degree scheme

2 Silly errors, haphazard grammar, and badly organised sentences – you will be spending a great deal of your time writing essays, so indicate that you possess the necessary skills

3 Oversimplifications, clichés and pat answers – a university degree is all about discussion, argument and debate

4 Getting names or book titles wrong – you should name names and be specific – but make sure that you get all the names or titles of books right in the first place!

RECOMMENDED READING AND WEBSITES

- Read American novels, historical works and read quality newspapers for current affairs in the USA
- British Association for American studies (www.bass.ac.uk)
- American studies links (www.americansc.org.uk)
- CRAC Degree Course Guide: *English, Media Studies and American Studies* Richmond; CRAC/Trotman Publishing, 2007
- I am grateful for the support of Swansea University (www.swan.ac.uk/ american) in the preparation of this profile.

ARCHAEOLOGY AND ANTHROPOLOGY

This academic profile was written using information provided by admissions tutors at Southampton University and focuses on archaeology as a single honours discipline. The information in this profile is useful to all applicants, but please be aware that some of the advice is pertinent to that department in particular.

 ## SUBJECT OVERVIEW

Archaeology is a subject that provides the opportunity to uncover past peoples and their worlds. From their material remains, you can find out about their daily lives: what they ate, what they wore and the kinds of landscapes they lived in. You can also find out about the 'big questions' about how society was organised, the scale of trade and exchange, belief structures and technology. Archaeology offers a unique blend of humanities and science, practical and theoretical. For this reason it offers excellent transferable skills which mean graduates can go into many careers.

It is quite often accompanied by anthropology as a joint honours option, although both subjects can also be studied separately as single honours degrees. Anthropology is often described as the comparative study of human societies. Social and cultural anthropology look mainly at contemporary societies, at what they have in common and what makes them different from one another. Biological anthropology is the study of human beings as a species, and includes hominid and primate evolution, primate behaviour, population genetics and demography, and forensic anthropology. Like archaeology, anthropology is an interdisciplinary subject, utilising scientific, social scientific and humanities theories, methods and perspectives.

WHAT SKILLS OR ATTRIBUTES DO ADMISSIONS TUTORS LOOK FOR IN A GOOD APPLICANT?

Archaeology A level is still taught by only a small number of colleges, so we do not have any specific subject requirements, and our students come from a diversity of paths: either all sciences, all arts, or a combination. For archaeological science and combined honours programmes, we do look for a good grade in specific appropriate subjects, and this would be true of most other departments. That being said, students who do study archaeology to A level would need to highlight what aspects of their work they have found most interesting and discuss their fieldwork opportunities and coursework plans.

More important is that you should be able to demonstrate an interest in finding out about the past, whether from excavation or museum experience, or from family holidays visiting British castles, or the ruins of Pompeii. We look for a questioning mind and enthusiasm, as evidenced by a good academic track record at A level and GCSE, and performance at interview.

As archaeology is largely about teamwork, we also look for ability to work as part of a team: you do not have to be the life and soul of the party, but you do need to be willing to participate and join in.

WHAT DOES A GOOD PERSONAL STATEMENT LOOK LIKE?

You should use your personal statement as an opportunity to show what you are interested in the study of the past. Only approximately 25% of applicants will have studied archaeology at AS or A2 level, so why do you want to study it at university? What stirred your interest – was it a childhood visit to an ancient monument, or a particular TV programme? What have you done to further that interest – visiting more sites in Britain and abroad, reading specific books, taking part on an excavation, or work experience in a museum? What skills do you have from your GCSEs and A levels, or from extracurricular activities, that prepare you for an archaeology degree? If you are applying for a combined honours degree, why do you want to do that particular combination?

TOP TIPS FOR A GOOD PERSONAL STATEMENT

1 Say what it is that excites you about the past

2 Mention specific sites and museums you have visited

3 If you are applying for a combined honours degree, say why you want to study both subjects together

4 If you have an interest in a particular aspect of archaeology – for example, Romans or animal bones – mention it

5 Be positive

6 Make sure that you present yourself in as compelling and interesting way as you can.

THINGS TO AVOID

1 Plagiarising your statement by downloading it from the web or copying it word for word from a book

2 Applying for combined honours in archaeology and history, and then only talking about how interested you are in history and failing to mention archaeology – we assume you will not get the grades for a history degree and are using the combined honours as a back door into the single honours

3 Spelling and grammatical mistakes in your personal statements

4 Saying anything about yourself which is not true – we usually find out at interview

5 Including left-field archaeological ideas – the Pyramids were *not* built by aliens!

RECOMMENDED READING AND WEBSITES

- Council for British Archaeology (www.britarch.ac.uk)
- *Current Archaeology* (www.archaeology.co.uk)
- *Current World Archaeology* (www.archaeology.co.uk)
- *British Archaeology* (www.britarch.ac.uk)
- I am grateful for the support of Southampton University (www.arch.soton. ac.uk) in the preparation of this profile.

BIOSCIENCES

This profile is a composite based on a variety of sources, including information provided by the primary source, Birmingham University. The information in this profile is useful to all applicants, but please be aware that some of the advice is pertinent to that department in particular.

SUBJECT OVERVIEW

The biosciences refer to a relatively new term for university departments that teach subjects with a biological base. As far as most undergraduates are concerned, they will normally find four different courses, each with their own demands and specialism. Biological sciences degrees are similar to biology A level courses – they are a natural progression from that. A Biochemistry degree (which is often linked with pharmacology), has a greater molecular content and normally expects both chemistry and biology to A level or their equivalent. Human biology (along with subjects such as anatomy) is self-explanatory and finally you have the new bioinformatics courses. These are cutting-edge degrees that specialise in the interplay between computer technology, nanotechnology and biology. For departments that offer this course, go to the UCAS course search facility.

WHAT SKILLS OR ATTRIBUTES DO ADMISSIONS TUTORS LOOK FOR IN A GOOD APPLICANT?

Essentially most good departments are looking for sound academic skills, commensurate with the demands of the course, and an interesting range of non-academic skills to complement the academic. Most tutors will look for evidence that the candidate has an aptitude for practical work, a demonstrable interest in science and how it affects society as a whole and the independent learning skills that are required at university. Non-academic skills might include a competence with IT, an interesting range of extracurricular interests (including, where possible, evidence of personal leadership or initiative) and a lively and enquiring mind.

WHAT DOES A GOOD PERSONAL STATEMENT LOOK LIKE?

The admissions team at Birmingham indicate that what they are looking for is that you show your enthusiasm for the subject. This advice seems appropriate for all departments.

Is there something that's triggered your interest in the subject – did you go to a lecture or have a really good biology teacher? Or if you've just read a book, mention that. But don't make it up. You don't have to have had that that 'eureka' moment – if it's just the subject you've loved at school, then say so. Try to explain what aspects of science education you have enjoyed the most and why. If you have completed coursework, tell us about that and what you learnt about independent learning techniques. If you are good at practical work – say so! Also mention aspects of non-science subjects that you enjoy and have gained skills from pursuing. For instance, English may have taught you to write well or ICT to use the full range of information technology techniques.

The other thing to say about personal statements is that if there's something unusual about your application then address it in your personal statement – explain it. For example, sometimes Birmingham see students who haven't got ideal A levels – and that's sometimes because they've developed in biology later or maybe after they've started their AS levels. If you explain yourself, the admissions tutors won't just think 'well you haven't got the right A levels' and move on to the next application. Instead they will take time to consider whether you could manage the course.

TOP TIPS FOR A GOOD PERSONAL STATEMENT

1 Make sure that you support your choice of course with relevant evidence that indicates that this choice is made in a measured and reasoned way

2 Provide evidence of wider reading beyond the standard A level specification to show that you are someone with a genuine passion for the subject

3 Promote yourself in a positive manner, accentuating your skills and attributes, both academic and non-academic

4 Make sure that you mention practical assessments, coursework or extended projects that you have completed to emphasise your ability to learn independently. This is a crucial skill at university.

THINGS TO AVOID

1 Careless spelling, grammar and punctuation errors

2 Lying about your achievements – this is often exposed at interview or elsewhere

3 Copying another person's personal statement – be inspired by them but do not lift chunks out of them!

4 Underselling yourself or writing in a verbose and uninspiring manner

5 Not showing any evidence of a genuine and sustained interest in biology or the biological sciences or telling us that you really wanted to be a doctor!

6 Indicating in your statement that you have a poor understanding of the demands of the subject, as a result of inadequate research.

RECOMMENDED READING AND WEBSITES

- CRAC Degree Course Guide: *Biological Sciences* Richmond; CRAC/ Trotman Publishing, 2006
- *New Scientist* (www.newscientist.com)
- *Nature* (www.nature.com)
- University of Warwick website has a useful science websites page – (www2. warwick.ac.uk/services/library/main/tealea/sciences/useful)
- I am grateful for the support of Birmingham University (www.bham.ac.uk) in the preparation of this profile.

BUSINESS AND MANAGEMENT

This academic profile was written using information provided by an admissions tutor at Aston University. The information is useful to all applicants, but some of the advice is pertinent to Aston in particular.

SUBJECT OVERVIEW

The practice of business and management (and all the other specialisms, such as accounting, marketing and economics) is a varied and fascinating subject and taking place around us every day. The globalised business and financial world and power of brands, finance, marketing, consumer behaviour, large organisations and multinationals along with the importance of entrepreneurship and forward thinking means a business degree is useful in many careers. Many business degrees include a fantastic opportunity to take a placement year in industry/commerce or work or study abroad as part of the course. Business students are a massively varied group of people, often from all over the world offering lots of new perspectives, friends and future contacts.

WHAT SKILLS OR ATTRIBUTES DO ADMISSIONS TUTORS LOOK FOR IN A GOOD APPLICANT?

We need to see evidence of commitment to a business and management degree, for instance a demonstrable interest in the business world. A good candidate would have an awareness of recent issues in the UK economy that are relevant, for instance the recent upheaval in the sub-prime market and its impact on banking and finance. Academic skills might be illustrated by a Business Studies or Economics A level or equivalent, but this is not always obligatory. Maths is another skill that is relevant, although the need for an A level will vary from course to course. A good candidate will show an awareness of globalisation, customer focus, organisations and how they work, the importance of brands and marketing, finance and economics. Non-academic skills might include good communication and teamwork skills, evidence of leadership or putting forward new ideas – for example from part-time or voluntary work. The Young Enterprise and Duke of Edinburgh's Award Schemes are both means of showing these attributes.

WHAT DOES A GOOD PERSONAL STATEMENT LOOK LIKE?

Make it clear and concise, clearly state why you want to study business, what your interests are and your specific subjects at school/college – for example, business, accounting, geography, economics – which you feel are relevant and worth talking about. Emphasise the relevant skills you have learnt and the books, newspapers and magazines that you have read to extend your understanding of the subject. You can see good examples below. You are encouraged to refer to demonstrable interests you might have in the business world. In this regard the Young Enterprise Scheme and other similar schemes are useful. Reference to current issues affecting business is always welcome.

TOP TIPS FOR A GOOD PERSONAL STATEMENT

1 Emphasise the skills that you have already acquired that are both academic and non-academic

2 Mention any work experience, business experience and/or taster courses that you have attended that may enhance your application

3 Read prospectuses and websites – business courses are different across the UK in how and what they teach and specialise in, and in how you are assessed. Your understanding of these needs to be reflected in your personal statements

THINGS TO AVOID

1 Repetition

2 Unsubstantiated claims that you could not defend in an interview

3 Poor spelling, punctuation and grammar. Check and read it carefully. You would be surprised how many errors we see that are the result of lazy proofreading or reliance on spell checks

4 Sweeping generalisations such as 'I have always been passionate about a career in. . .' – this is rarely true!

5 Choosing a university or particular course just because it is high in the league tables or your parents/

4 Do your research in plenty of time during March–July of Year 12 or equivalent – ready to complete and send off your UCAS form well before Christmas in Year 13 or equivalent. Early research also helps to establish enough time to prepare your statement properly.

teachers think it makes them look good – choose a university because you think the course content, reputation, graduate employability, teaching and social facilities are right for you. If appropriate you might indicate that you have done this in the body of your statement. Do not mention individual universities, but do indicate in general terms that you have done your research

6 Assuming we know all about you – we can't check you out on Facebook or YouTube – all we have is the UCAS form. So use it to sell yourself!

7 Using humour or crass statements on your personal statement – keep it concise, serious and realistic but positive.

RECOMMENDED READING AND WEBSITES

- CRAC Degree Course Guide: *Business and Economics,* Richmond; CRAC/Trotman Publishing, 2007.
- *The Financial Times* (www.ft.com): excellent source for business economics. Also contains a portfolio service for you to build your own virtual share portfolio and track your wealth
- *The Economist* (www.economist.com): web version of the weekly newspaper – lots of political economy, with a libertarian slant. Some articles are only available for those with subscription
- Business/finance pages of papers like *The Guardian*, *The Times*, *The Independent* and *The Daily Telegraph* to get a range of perspectives.
- *Marketing Week* (www.marketingweek.co.uk)
- The World Bank (www.worldbank.org): a detailed starting point for information and analysis of development issues

- Oneworld (www.oneworld.net): source of information on world economic events, giving an alternative view to that of the World Bank and International Monetary Fund (IMF)
- The Bank of England (www.bankofengland.co.uk): good source of information about macroeconomic policy in the UK, specially designed for A level students
- I am grateful for the support received from Aston University (www.abs.aston. ac.uk) in the preparation of this profile.

CLASSICS

(Classics, Classical Studies, Ancient History, Classical Archaeology)

This academic profile was written using information provided by an admissions tutor at King's College, University of London. The information is useful to all applicants, but some of the advice is pertinent to King's College, University of London in particular.

SUBJECT OVERVIEW

The cultures of the ancient world, embracing everything from the palaces of Bronze Age Crete to Roman cities on the African frontier – are fascinating to study in their own right. But because classical texts and art have significantly influenced thought, literature and politics since ancient times, they also offer a skeleton key to understanding much of Western culture.

Classics, classical studies, ancient history and classical archaeology make up a family of degree programmes offering different avenues of approach to ancient cultures, via their languages and literature (in the original or in translation), their political, military and cultural history, their material remains, and their effects on later times.

Although each individual programme has its own specific focus and methods, they also offer the possibility of combining a diverse range of subjects: classicists may combine historical and archaeological courses with their work on Homer, Virgil, and tragedy; ancient historians may move between Herodotus, Hadrian's Wall and lyric poetry; and classical studies students might look at the early Iron Age alongside their Ovid. To students who have studied classical subjects at school, the university curriculum offers a new range of subjects spanning ideas, objects and areas of which they may have been completely unaware before.

A classics-related degree has the advantage of being very highly regarded by employers, while offering an unpredictable and interesting course of study. Students often travel with their subject, venturing through the modern countries of the Mediterranean, Europe and the Middle East with the eye of an informed explorer. These are the original interdisciplinary degrees, offering the opportunity to experience cutting-edge methods and approaches for historical, literary and archaeological study more generally.

WHAT SKILLS OR ATTRIBUTES DO ADMISSIONS TUTORS LOOK FOR IN A GOOD APPLICANT?

As a good classics applicant you will have the same general skills and attributes as any good humanities applicant: enthusiasm, self-motivation, a desire to learn, an appetite both for different perspectives and for challenging questions. The King's College London admissions team hope to see applicants who enjoy independently exploring new topics, whether in the library, the museum, or the field; people who want to engage with new problems and techniques, and to get behind the clichés of mass-media versions of ancient myth and conflict. This is an approach that will be mirrored in similar departments elsewhere.

Because of their different angles of approach, the different degree programmes within classics do not all call for exactly the same skills and strengths; there are variations in emphasis from one university department to another. In particular, it is a good idea for applicants without an ancient language to check what quantity of work in classical Greek or Latin a particular programme is going to expect.

Departments that require compulsory language work from all their students want to see evidence that you have some aptitude and interest in learning languages. If you have been lucky enough to acquire ancient languages at school, bear in mind that university assessment will require more extended commentary and essay writing in all topics, so the ability to write as well as translate fluently is key.

Departments recruiting for degrees in classical archaeology will also prefer candidates with an ability to look carefully at visual evidence and to produce some ideas about how material objects may be used to reconstruct the ancient world. Admissions staff for both archaeology and ancient history will be interested in how analytically you can think about evidence and piece together your ideas based on it.

Depending on the university's balance between individual and group teaching, universities may look for evidence that you will be a responsive student, willing to voice your opinion in a group, or to discuss your ideas with the lecturer and with fellow students. Your key qualities are enthusiasm and motivation.

WHAT DOES A GOOD PERSONAL STATEMENT LOOK LIKE?

Remember who you are talking to in your statement: the admissions tutor is a member of the academic staff whose job it is to let in students who s/he thinks s/he and her/his colleagues will find interesting and enjoyable to teach and have in their department. So sell yourself first and foremost as a sparky, intelligent, interestingly teachable enthusiast for the subject(s) you are applying for. Everything else is secondary, however brilliant your sporting record, your Young Enterprise achievements, or your tap-dancing.

Try to be individual without going over the top. If you suspect lots of other people are going to be saying what you are thinking of saying (for example, 'I've always been interested in the ancient world, ever since I first opened a book of Greek myths'), then either don't say it, or find some individual slant (for example, a particular myth, and problem it sets you, or the insight it gives you into the world of the Greeks). Try to avoid clichés and verdicts that sound as if you are only delivering them because you think it's expected, or because that's what you were told to say in an A level essay ('In my reading I have much enjoyed exploring the contrast between Catullus' coarse invective and the rhetorical wit of Ovid.'). You should aim to *demonstrate* your skills and interests rather than just stating them, through specific examples.

Show that you have got a sense of the questions that are there to be asked, and the new territory you will be able to explore at university, (but without becoming just mistily aspirational – this will just put them off). It is fine to talk about your extracurricular activities and successes, but try to make sure that what you say helps to show that you have the kinds of skill (like time management) that will also help you make a success of your studies and be an asset to the department.

If you have not been able to study the ancient world at school (for example, A/S or A level work in ancient history or classical civilisation), it is important to show through other evidence that you are a suitable and interesting candidate. Demonstrate that you have an intelligent interest from activity outside formal study. This might include reading of Greek and Roman history and literature (preferably including ancient texts in translation, rather than only modern works of popular history);visits to archaeological sites and museums; and interest in ancient remains in Greece and Italy (and other relevant parts of the world, even if you have not managed to visit yet). Mention specifics – works of ancient literature, or of historical analysis, or places that you have found particularly intriguing – *and say why*. These may be followed up in interviews, so make sure that your interest is genuine!

You should also try to explain how the work you have done at school, even if not directly focused on the ancient world, has nevertheless equipped you, in terms of approach, to tackle the ancient world. You do not have to apologise for not (yet) knowing any Latin or Greek – most students in classical studies, ancient history and classical archaeology will be starting in exactly the same position.

Your personal statement is also the place to explain anything unusual in your qualifications so far. If you need to, give good reasons to show that your formal results so far give a misleading picture of your real abilities. Tutors know that accidents happen in exams, and are very ready to listen to well-documented explanations.

Examples from specific personal statements (from King's College, London)

From candidates who have studied ancient languages at school:

> I have loved Latin since I began it at the age of nine.

✓ It is encouraging that you still enjoy ancient languages after lengthy study, and your background in the subject will stand you in good stead for university. You could add that you have been looking in new directions for your university career. What authors have you read and would you like to go on to read? How do you think they may fit in the wider history of the ancient world? Are there any themes (death and mourning, involvement in politics, descriptions of remote places) in the texts that you have read which you would like to explore further?

From candidates who have little school background in the study of the ancient world:

> My interest was first sparked by the myths of Greece and Rome. . . I am very interested in ancient warfare and the conquests of Alexander the Great.

✓ Your attention has, understandably, been attracted by certain prominent stories and figures and this is appreciated by the admissions tutor. But if you're considering studying this at university, try to contextualise the images you have of the ancient world more. What have you read in ancient texts about warfare? What further questions might you go on to ask about Alexander the Great? Is there a course at your preferred university which covers this period and which will offer you more?

From a candidate interested in classical archaeology:

> In my gap year, I will be studying for a foundation course in art at X Art School. I am interested in all periods of art history and I would particularly like to study the relationship between ancient sculpture and Renaissance art.
>   Coming to the study of archaeology with a background in art, rather than science, can produce interesting and equally valid approaches. Your dedication to a whole year of fine art study will suggest to the admissions tutor that you might work well with visual analysis and respond in interesting ways to the ancient evidence. There can be very different kinds of archaeological study, however, and an interviewer might be interested in to what extent you're aware of this. An interest in art history would also be balanced by the practical experience of a British dig, for which you could volunteer.

TOP TIPS FOR A GOOD PERSONAL STATEMENT

1 Be *intelligently* enthusiastic

2 Make sure you know the details of the programmes you are applying for and that this is reflected in the body of the text

3 Keep your personal statement focused on what will make you a rewarding student of your chosen subject

4 Read through what you have written and correct it where necessary

5 Back up what you say about yourself with evidence, from extended reading, fieldwork or other sources. Be prepared to defend yourself if called to interview

6 If your choice of subject is a recent one and you have not had years to construct a relevant extracurricular CV, you can provide an equally encouraging and impressive substitute in your statement by talking in detail about relevant background reading and by describing the further preparatory study you may undertake – perhaps a summer school, independent language study (with course book), visits to local Roman sites or more exotic climes or volunteer work in a museum or site. The more detailed and worked-out these plans are, the better.

THINGS TO AVOID

1 Being too vague in your explanations of interest – try to get to the point quickly and back it up

2 Parroting second-hand opinions

3 Going on at great length about activities and achievements that are irrelevant to your chosen course.

RECOMMENDED READING AND WEBSITES

- Archaeological excavations of interest to classics: (www.indiana. edu/~classics/AIA/internet/internet.html)
- Classics at Oxford (www.classics.ox.ac.uk)
- Classics at Durham (www.dur.ac.uk/classics)
- Warwick University (ww2.warwick.ac.uk/services/library/main/tealea/arts/ classics/usefulwebsites)
- I am grateful for the support I received from King's College London (www .kcl.ac.uk/schools/humanities/classics) In preparing this profile.

COMPUTER SCIENCE

This profile was written using information from an admissions tutor at Royal Holloway, University of London. The information is useful to all applicants, but some of the advice is pertinent to that department in particular.

SUBJECT OVERVIEW

Computers, the internet, the web and other digital technologies continue to transform the economy, the world of finance and many other aspects of society. This digital revolution is accelerating and will play a key role in shaping the future. Computer science lies at the heart of this transformation: it studies how any sort of information, whether it is music or biological sequence data, can be represented and processed digitally. Demand for good computer science graduates has never been higher: a degree in computer science equips you for many challenging, and sometimes very well paid jobs in fields like finance, computational biology and many areas of business. Research by the eSkills sector skills council for IT and telecoms shows that the employment market for IT careers is growing five times faster than the general economy; every year 140,000 new entrants to the IT and telecoms workforce are needed.

Computer science is an excellent preparation for many careers, both technical and non-technical, throughout commerce and industry because students acquire intellectual discipline and practical project completion skills, which are highly valued, as well as specific technical skills that are in great demand. These include:

- The ability to analyse complex problems
- The ability to acquire the skills needed to solve problems and to design and implement solutions
- Programming skills, including networking and databases
- Data analysis skills
- Communication skills
- The ability to work in a team
- Leadership skills and management ability
- Literacy and numeracy
- Presentation skills.

If you would like to drive future technological developments, a degree in computer science will provide the necessary knowledge and practical experience to help you achieve your ambitions.

 ## WHAT SKILLS AND ATTRIBUTES DO ADMISSIONS TUTORS LOOK FOR IN A GOOD APPLICANT?

Computer science is a hard but rewarding discipline. Admissions tutors generally tend to look for students who have some sort of technical or mathematical background. Students without an A level (or equivalent) in a technical subject like maths, physics or economics often struggle with the more abstract thinking required in computer science. Most first years have no previous experience with programming but if students have some programming experience in a language, for example C++ or Visual Basic, that is not just a markup or scripting language that is a good selling point. Tutors also tend to look for some interest or enthusiasm for computers, even if this is quite general.

In terms of academic qualifications, departments vary and you need to do your research. However, as a general rule the better departments will expect grades of between AAB and BBB and most good candidates will have studied AS or A level Maths. Computer Science or ICT AS level and the other mainstream sciences are also preferred. However, do your research carefully to ascertain what each department requires.

Tutors want students who have the maturity and self-discipline to cope with the more autonomous nature of university life; students need to be able to manage their time, and balance the demands of the different courses. Students also need to be problem solvers; they need to be curious and independent minded. Students can show they have these personal qualities through the range of their extracurricular activities or part-time work.

WHAT DOES A GOOD PERSONAL STATEMENT LOOK LIKE?

This statement is a composite of various personal statements:

I have always been very interested in computers. When I was a child, I would often take things apart to see how they work. When I was 10 years old, I was given a computer for my birthday, and while I started off just playing games and so on with it, I soon became more interested in trying to understand how it worked. At first I just would write little macros in Visual Basic to do useful things, but then I taught myself Java, and have written some simple games using this as part of my school computer club. I am also very interested in graphics and Photoshopping pictures to make them more interesting. I have made several websites using PHP and CSS, and I spend a lot of time reading about computers on the web and in magazines. My current computer I built myself from parts, which was a very educational experience, especially as it didn't work to start off with and I had to figure out why.

I have a part-time job at PC World, where I work as part of a team providing technical support for customers. My hobbies include playing the piano for a number of years, and I have achieved Grade 5. I play sometimes in a band with some friends. My other main interest is sport, especially cricket. I have been part of the school team for several years.

Academically, I have always been interested in Maths, and with my love of computers, computer science seems a natural choice. I chose Maths and Physics as two of my A levels, but not computing as I didn't enjoy ICT much at GCSE level, because the course focussed just on using programs rather than making them.

I am hard working and well organised, and think I will be able to cope well with the demands of a hard degree like CS: I am looking forward to the challenges of university life, and I want to get a job working in IT when I graduate.

This is a good personal statement, as the student gives some reasons why he wants to study CS, and illustrates his enthusiasm for the subject with concrete examples. He shows he has self-discipline, takes part in a range of activities and has a serious interest in computing.

 **TOP TIPS FOR A GOOD PERSONAL STATEMENT**

1 Make sure that you emphasise your ability in the technical or mathematical subjects

2 If you enjoy puzzles, chess, card games such as poker or bridge and mental arithmetic puzzles such as Sudoku, let us know

3 If you have knowledge of programming, even at a fairly basic level, please let us know and tell us about programmes you have written and why

4 If you are studying computer science at school, tell us what you particularly enjoyed that led you to apply for a degree level qualification. Read one of the suggested books and mention what you learnt from the book

5 Sell yourself in a compelling and interesting manner: write clearly and concisely.

 **THINGS TO AVOID**

1 Spelling and punctuation mistakes

2 Lying or plagiarism

3 Underselling your achievements

4 Telling us you are only interested in gaming – you may be but this should be counterbalanced with your other interests.

RECOMMENDED READING AND WEBSITES

- David Harel and Yishai Feldman, *Algorithmics: The Spirit of Computing*, Harlow, Addison-Wesley, 2004
- Douglas R Hofstadter, *Godel, Escher, Bach: An Eternal Golden Braid*, Harmondsworth, Penguin Books, 2000
- Eric S Raymond, *The Cathedral and the Bazaar: Musings on Linux and Open Source*, O'Reilly Media, 2001
- Cliff Stoll, *The Cuckoo's Egg: Tracking a Spy Through the Maze of Computer Espionage, Pocket Books*, 2005
- I am grateful for the support I received from Royal Holloway (www.cs.rhul. ac.uk) in the composition of this profile.

DRAMA AND THEATRE

This academic profile was written using information provided by an admissions tutor at Royal Holloway, University of London. The information is useful to all applicants, but some of the advice is pertinent to that department in particular.

SUBJECT OVERVIEW

Drama is a much sought-after and stimulating degree programme. It is the study of performance, and performance pervades all aspects of public and private existence. Performance is also about communication and we live in a society where communications are vitally important. Studying drama at university explores human interaction both in the present and in the past. It is an ancient art form of social practice, through which we can develop an understanding of society today. Drama as a form of cultural practice offers ways in which to express ideas about human life.

Students explore these through a variety of modes of study, active as well as sedentary, group-based as well as individual, spoken and as well as written, analytical as well as creative.

The study of drama and theatre provides you with useful life and employment skills, because of its emphasis on teamwork, planning projects, rigorous research and imaginative presentation.

A degree programme aims to teach as full a range of skills as possible, from the academic expertise of research and theoretical reading and writing to practical theatre skills. Students develop an inquisitive and questioning attitude to all aspects of the discipline. Specifically, students will gain skills in a variety of communications: writing logbooks and more traditional essays, presenting seminars, listening to peers' presentations and being able to pinpoint arguments that need further teasing out, and presenting performance work. Written skills in essay writing, logbook entries, review writing and bibliographic skills are also taught and assessed. Analytical skills in close textual reading, theoretical application, and performance analysis are also gained. The skills of a drama graduate are easily transferable to other environments and are therefore highly sought after by employers.

WHAT SKILLS AND ATTRIBUTES DO ADMISSIONS TUTORS LOOK FOR IN A GOOD APPLICANT?

Admissions tutors look for someone who has the ability to question. They are not looking for 'knowledge' of the subject because that merely tells them about the teaching that a candidate has received up to this point and not about the candidate themselves. So they are looking for potential.

Candidates need to demonstrate an interest in theatre, but this does not have to be in performing. Many university courses in drama are not concerned with developing acting abilities but rather fostering skills in group work, analysis, cultural engagement, and the bringing together of theoretical and practical exploration.

Admissions tutors like candidates who are good group members: this might be shown socially by the range of activities the student undertakes. They are also looking to match students to courses: for example, someone who wants to train to be an actor would be better applying for those courses; many university courses are about studying drama in a wider context and would be frustrating for those who want specialist training (and have perhaps applied to academic university courses because their parents want them to).

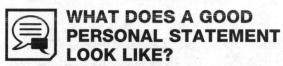

WHAT DOES A GOOD PERSONAL STATEMENT LOOK LIKE?

Example of a good personal statement

I wish to study theatre/performance at university due to the passion I have for drama. What evokes this passion is the unique way drama allows exploration of the human condition, its history, its philosophies and beliefs and emotions therein. My enthusiasm has developed through practical investigation of Miller, Fo, Shakespeare, Brecht and more recently, Artaud and Grotowski. My understanding of Theatre has been greatly enhanced by my English Literature A level studies, through which I have broadened my knowledge of theatre history and revolutionary playwrights such as Marlowe. My understanding of photography has helped me to be creative and expressive in my work ad to use imagery effectively. This has aided my study of drama, particularly in devised work. At university I desire to continue to learn, explore and further develop my performance skills and my understanding of the world of Theatre.

I have aspirations to teach drama or to work in theatre. In the light of this I have applied for a nine-month placement in Tanzania teaching English and drama in African schools. I feel participating in such a scheme will help me to mature further and develop communication skills and subject knowledge. I am a very self-motivated person who enjoys getting involved in extracurricular activities. For example, in November I played Ophelia in the school production of 'Hamlet'. During this process I gained a greater appreciation of how the theatre works and how much effort goes into putting on a show. This understanding was further developed in April when I was given the role of deputy stage manager in a school production of The 'Threepenny Opera'. I am also a member of the school chamber choir and jazz choir.

✓ This statement shows someone who can think about the importance of drama within a wider context; the candidate is able to think about some of the functions of drama and also how their other A levels have broadened their understanding. The gap year activities are pertinent to the subject and challenging. The candidate's interest in drama goes beyond acting or self-interest: the lead female role in Hamlet provided a chance to think more about production aspects. The candidate shows that social activities have developed a sense of group membership.

TOP TIPS FOR A GOOD PERSONAL STATEMENT

1 Indicate that you are aware that drama and theatre studies at university tend to combine the academic study of theatre with performance skills.
Some courses place very little emphasis on performance. You need to express clearly that you understand the distinction between performance arts and theatre studies and make it clear that you believe that this is right for you

2 Illustrate your experience of performance with reference to live acts you have seen and how they have extended your knowledge of the subject

3 Talk about the skills you have learnt from your study of drama or theatre studies thus far

4 Emphasise the fact that you are personally motivated and willing to work hard independently to achieve your goals

5 Detail the non-academic interests you have especially if they involve working in an environment that promotes personal leadership and the need to overcome challenges without direct adult control, for instance the Duke of Edinburgh's Award.

THINGS TO AVOID

1 Poorly constructed sentences with no clear direction or purpose

2 Spelling, grammar and punctuation errors

3 A statement that indicates that you have little understanding of the demands of the course and an awareness of the distinction between acting and drama/ theatre studies

4 Making any claims that you would struggle to defend if called to interview or audition – that means no barefaced lies or blatant plagiarism of statements you might find on the internet. Be yourself!

RECOMMENDED READING AND WEBSITES

- CRAC Degree Course Guide: *Music, Drama and Dance*, Richmond: CRAC/ Trotman Publishing, 2007
- The writings by practitioners such as Peter Brook or Augusto Boal are accessible and help shed light on different aspects of theatre
- Alison Hodge, *Twentieth Century Actor Training*, London: Routledge, 2000
- Emma Govan, Helen Nicholson and Katie Normington, *Making a Performance: Devising Histories and Contemporary Practices,* London: Routledge, 2007
- David Wiles, *A Short History of Western Performance Space,* Cambridge: Cambridge University Press, 2003
- I am grateful for the support of Royal Holloway (www.rhul.ac.uk/drama) in the preparation of this profile.

ENGINEERING (CIVIL)

This academic profile was written using information provided by an admissions tutor at Southampton University and focuses on civil engineering as a single honours discipline. Engineering as a discipline at university is varied in its focus. Courses on offer include mechanical, aeronautical, structural, electrical and civil engineering. Each deal with a different aspect of human engineering needs and will require different skills, academic qualifications and interests. The information here is useful to all applicants, but some of the advice is pertinent to Southampton in particular.

SUBJECT OVERVIEW

Civil engineering applies science, mathematics, design and creativity to solve problems of critical importance to society, across construction, maintenance and management of infrastructure. We tend to take for granted the buildings we live and work in, the roads, railways and airports that allow us to travel, and the water that we use. It is professional civil engineers who make all this possible, and who are called on to find solutions to the major challenges facing the world in the future, such as the effects of climate change and sea level rise, finding sustainable sources of energy and dealing with congestion.

These degree courses provide excellent preparation, in terms of knowledge and understanding and key transferable skills, for a career in civil engineering. Many courses are fully accredited by the Institution of Civil Engineers and the Institution of Structural Engineers, providing the first stage in a recognised career path to Chartered or Incorporated Engineer status. Employment prospects are excellent.

WHAT SKILLS AND ATTRIBUTES DO ADMISSIONS TUTORS LOOK FOR IN A GOOD APPLICANT?

The essential academic skills we look for are numeracy, problem solving ability and logical thinking. Most entry requirements therefore include A level Mathematics and a science, or equivalent qualifications. We also look for good communication skills in our students, both written and verbal. Other positive attributes are IT skills, a practical hands-on attitude to situations, and design flair and creativity, particularly for the civil engineering with architecture course.

Important personal qualities for a professional engineer are teamworking skills and leadership ability, evidence of potential for which we can look for in candidates' personal statements, where they describe sporting activities, clubs, societies, hobbies, voluntary activities or business games in which they have been actively involved.

WHAT DOES A GOOD PERSONAL STATEMENT LOOK LIKE ?

Explain why you wish to pursue the particular line of study: Here we would expect to see some brief background on why you wish to pursue a career in civil engineering. This could be related to a family link, for example working in the family's construction business, or other experiences, for instance seeing structures while on holiday, articles in books/journals/ engineering press, work experience.

Describe the efforts you have already made to further your knowledge and understanding in the area: Good applications always describe what steps the candidate has taken to find out more about the subject area. This is best done through practical experiences in the form of work experience placements with engineering firms, attending guest lectures, or participating in an Engineering Head Start course at a university. You should briefly describe what you got out of the experience and how it has influenced you to apply for the course.

Describe other attributes that demonstrate your wider 'generic' skills set: Describe any relevant work experience you have had and how it has improved your communication, negotiation and team building skills, for example, care in the community, shop work, engineering placements. Sporting achievements, clubs and society memberships, vocational qualifications and particularly any positions of responsibility taken within those areas should be highlighted, for example being a member of a football team, Duke of Edinburgh's Awards. Any charity work can also be mentioned.

Link your generic skills set to the needs of your chosen course: A good personal statement will go that step further and state how the skills learned through your generic skills will benefit you during your course, for instance, leadership or teamworking skills gained through a part-time job or while on a charity bike ride could help in undergraduate group projects or on a work placement.

TOP TIPS FOR A GOOD PERSONAL STATEMENT

1 Present all your qualifications clearly and accurately

2 Write a succinct and clear personal statement, with a clear direction and flow from one point

THINGS TO AVOID

1 Ambiguous or missing information

2 Spelling or grammatical errors

3 Thinking that engineering is about fixing things such as washing machines or cars

to another. Keep it concise and precise, promoting your skills in a compelling and interesting way

3 Demonstrate your understanding of what engineering is about, preferably drawing on examples of engineering that you have read about or personally experienced. What motivated your interest in this subject?

4 Demonstrate you are interested in applying maths and science to real problems – mention the fact that you enjoy puzzles, mental arithmetic and designing

5 Demonstrate in your statement activities that you have taken part in that show team working and leadership skills.

4 Saying that you can't wait to move away from anything involving maths and science

5 Saying that your favourite hobby is going out with friends or watching the television – this is too often repeated and appears lazy and ill-prepared.

 ## RECOMMENDED READING AND WEBSITES

- CRAC Degree Course Guide: *Engineering*, Richmond; CRAC/Trotman Publishing, 2007
- *New Civil Engineer* (www.nce.co.uk)
- *Construction News* (www.cnplus.co.uk)
- Institution of Civil Engineers (www.ice.org.uk)
- I am grateful to Southampton University (www.ses.soton.ac.uk) for their support in the preparation of this profile.

ENGLISH

This academic profile was written using information provided by admissions tutors at Royal Holloway, University of London University and Queen Mary's, University of London (QMUL). Most of the information was provided by the former and information provided by the latter is clearly indicated in the profile. The information is useful to all applicants, but some of the advice is pertinent to Royal Holloway and Queen Mary's in particular.

SUBJECT OVERVIEW

English is a versatile and interesting subject, characterised by the rigorous critical study of literature and language. It is concerned with the production, reception and interpretation of written texts, and with the literary and expressive potential of the English language. The study of English demands a constant commitment to improving your reading and writing skills. It develops a flexible and responsive openness of mind and advanced skills in argument, and encourages you to think critically for yourself about literature and life.

In the first year most students take a common set of courses that introduce them to some of the major areas of literary study and provide them with an historical understanding of literature that stretches back as far as medieval times. This gives students the basis to progress to more advanced, specialised study of particular areas. In the second and third years, students are able to choose from a number of optional courses as wide ranging as science fiction to Afro-American literature.

It is *vital* to research each department carefully and find out what they expect from you. If you love American literature, then do not apply to a department with no particular interest in that genre. This lazy approach will often lead to rejection in what is a very competitive application process.

A degree in English trains the mind and feeds the imagination; it provides a range of transferable skills, including oral and written presentation skills, time management, and the ability to work independently, all of which are valued by employers. Most importantly, it also leaves your options open to pursue a career of your choice.

WHAT SKILLS AND ATTRIBUTES DO ADMISSIONS TUTORS LOOK FOR IN A GOOD APPLICANT?

Admissions tutors will always consider the level of attainment in GCSEs and predicted grades for A levels first of all. Many English courses now demand very high grades, simply due to supply and demand. It is not at all uncommon for candidates to be made offers of AAB or higher. Equally, it is not unusual for candidates to be rejected from one or more of their preferred universities. However, it is also possible to get into English courses with lower grades. Do your research carefully!

The personal statement and school reference are then read for any signs that interest in English is not just a narrow product of quite enjoying it at A level. Tutors would hope to see indications of longstanding enjoyment, and an understanding that English at university will not be like three more years of A level English, but will be more demanding and unpredictable. We want to see evidence of wide reading and an appreciation of different literary genres.

Good applicants demonstrate excellent academic potential, demonstrated by their strong A level or equivalent grades, and enthusiasm for further study. They show good time management and teamwork skills; the one to manage independent study successfully, the other to work co-operatively in seminars and group projects.

WHAT DOES A GOOD PERSONAL STATEMENT LOOK LIKE?

A good personal statement introduces your real passions and personality. Just as every student is different, so every statement should also be different. However, more successful statements will demonstrate a sincere love of literature that goes beyond the set texts at school. Cultural interests, widely defined, should appear such as theatre-going, gallery-visiting, films and music (if applicable).

> **During August, I volunteered to work as a literacy support assistant at my local library.**

✓ This is an example of real commitment to literature. The applicant saw reading as something of such utility and social value, that she was helping others to begin.

Good statements also make it clear that the candidate wants to study literature and is interested in the kind of programme offered at a particular university.

QMUL also stresses the importance of the personal statement, which will help determine whether an applicant will be offered an interview. According to Dr Reid, a senior admissions tutor, your statement should illustrate dedication and enthusiasm to the subject area. He looks in particular for:

....

 . . . an indication of intellectual and cultural interests, along with evidence of commitment to the subject area, and liveliness and independence of mind. **ᐧ**

He also makes the point that for a department which interviews applicants, an effective personal statement is especially important because, more often than not:

....

We use this part of the UCAS application as a starting point for discussion during the academic interview. **ᐧ**

Dr Cornelia Cook, Head of Admissions for English, says that they are looking for 'evidence of wide and engaged reading', and ultimately, a real commitment to the subject. And finally, if you do not want to be humiliated at interview (and not many applicants do), you need to be prepared to discuss anything mentioned in your personal statement, including any texts. This could prove tricky if you have exaggerated your achievements and/or fabricated hobbies to make yourself sound more interesting.

TOP TIPS FOR A GOOD PERSONAL STATEMENT

1 The personal statement is an important discriminatory tool and therefore it should be prepared with care and attention to detail

2 Emphasise early on a genuine passion for literature, reinforcing this with evidence that you have read widely and beyond the remit of the A level syllabus. If you mention an author you must be prepared to discuss this author's work if called to interview!

3 Admissions tutors look for clear evidence of liveliness and independence of mind

4 Clearly express the skills that you have learnt from the study of English and other subjects to A level or their equivalent

5 Tell the tutor about the extracurricular pursuits you enjoy, but avoid just listing them. Concentrate on one or two activities that you feel particularly passionate about, and then tell then why and what you have learnt from the pursuit of these activities

6 Read as widely as possible, in particular other works by the authors you are studying, beyond the set texts. Experiencing performances of classic theatre, such as Shakespeare, or opera, would be beneficial.

THINGS TO AVOID

1 Poor spelling, punctuation, grammar and sentence construction. This is English after all!

2 Failing to express your passion for English and not reinforcing it with examples that go beyond the remit of your A level course

3 Exaggerating your achievements and/or making up hobbies to make you sound more interesting – if you do not want to be humiliated at interview, you need to be prepared to discuss anything mentioned in your personal statement: including any texts.

RECOMMENDED READING AND WEBSITES

- CRAC Degree Course Guide: *English, Media Studies & American Studies*, Richmond: CRAC/Trotman Publishing, 2007.
- Explore some of the major works of pre-20th century literature – novelists such as Henry Fielding, Jane Austen, George Eliot, Charles Dickens; poets such as Donne, Wordsworth, Coleridge and Keats.
- I am grateful to the English departments at Queen Mary's (www.english. qmul.ac.uk) and Royal Holloway (www.rhul.ac.uk/english) for their support in compiling this profile.

ENVIRONMENTAL SCIENCE

This profile was written using information provided by an admissions tutor at Southampton University. Environmental science as a discipline is offered in a variety of different guises. These include single honours courses, environmental earth sciences, geophysical sciences and environmental geography. Each relates to a different aspect of this branch of science and will require different skills, academic qualifications and interests. The information here is useful to all applicants, but some of the advice is pertinent to Southampton in particular.

SUBJECT OVERVIEW

Environmental sciences directly addresses the major and pressing issues facing human beings and the world we live in. Such problems have become regular headline news items over the last few years and include climate change, tsunamis, deforestation, pollution, destruction of wildlife, earthquakes and genetically modified organisms (GMOs).

At the same time it allows students to study for an interdisciplinary degree, cutting across the boundaries between traditional science subjects like biology, chemistry, geography, geology and oceanography, usually with a large practical and field-based element.

This is a growing area of career employment opportunity and the skills of an environmental scientist can now be used in many fields in the private and public sector.

Most degrees are modular, with a series of modules taken each year, building annually to increase the specialisation and complexity. Students often take a residential field course in Year 1 to develop practical skills and can take a further residential field course in Year 3, which is more student-led, involving extensive field data collection and reporting.

WHAT SKILLS OR ATTRIBUTES DO ADMISSIONS TUTORS LOOK FOR IN A GOOD APPLICANT?

Academic skills include communication (oral and written), team skills, numeracy and some evidence of scientific practical skill is normally preferred. Non-academic skills include Independence, commitment and resilience.

The A level requirements vary from department to department. However, as a general rule most good departments will expect grades of between AAB and BBC. They will almost certainly expect at least one Science A2 level (or equivalent) with preference given to biology and chemistry. Other good subjects include maths, geography, geology and physics.

WHAT DOES A GOOD PERSONAL STATEMENT LOOK LIKE?

Demonstrate your knowledge and enthusiasm: say why you really want to do this degree, what has inspired you and why. If you have been involved in any relevant activities, through school or college, or perhaps through voluntary work, you should tell us about that, too. Do tell admissions tutors about other things as well. If you are interested in sport or music that's fine and achievement in non-academic areas can impress and show you are a good all-rounder. But focus mainly on your interest in the degree, and why this is what you want to do, including any aspirations for future careers.

Example of a good personal statement

The environment is something I have always been passionate about. From an early age I have watched wildlife in our garden, observing the annual cycles of life. At the same time I have always been committed to taking positive steps to help our environment – getting my parents to recycle their newspapers and switching to low energy light bulbs when I was still at primary school. Since then my knowledge has expanded and my commitment has grown. I was chairman of a student group that helped my school gain EcoSchool status in 2006, and I was co-ordinator of our conservation group, creating a nature trail in the school grounds and working as volunteers on local nature reserves. I am also a member of my local Friends of the Earth group, and have been actively involved in their recent campaigns about overfishing, including attending a large demonstration in London.

✓ This demonstrates long-term commitment to issues relevant to the degree.

My inspiration has increasingly come from my studies and the reading I have done to support them. I have immersed myself in the works of Aldo Leopold such as 'Sand County Almanac' – although these were written in the first half of the last century the lessons about prudent use of our world's resources apply more than ever today.

✓ Good evidence of academic commitment and knowledge, well written.

Inspired by work such as that, and by the global leadership of Al Gore and the Intergovernmental Panel on Climate Change, I now want to study for a degree that will both challenge me intellectually and lead to a worthwhile and rewarding career.
    I chose my A levels in Chemistry, Geography and Biology with an environmental sciences degree in mind. I enjoy practical work, both in the laboratory and in the field, and put them to good use in a work placement last summer in the Environment Agency's laboratories, analysing water quality.

✓ Relevant to this type of course, and an indication of skills.

Our field trip to Belize changed my life – the wealth of environmental riches in Latin America is truly astounding – with coral reefs, rainforests and wildlife, as well as remarkable local cultures – but the threats they may face in future years from the activities of humans is alarming.

✓ Good example, nicely summarised.

I hope one day to work in research into managing conservation areas in developing countries, and have taken Spanish AS level this year to help develop some useful language skills.

✓ Shows forward planning, strategic thinking and some ambitious career aspirations.

> I am a member of my local football team, and have been captain for the last two years, which has given me additional responsibility in getting everyone to work together – we were the first girls' team set up in our town and have been together for five years, and won the County Cup in 2007. I take an interest the arts as well – I play jazz piano in a band at college and we have performed in local music festivals. I hope to continue some sports and music at university.

✓ Evidence of ability as a team player, also of self-management.

Example of a poor personal statement

> I think an environmental sciences degree would be really good for me to study. It will be really interesting to find out more about our world.

✗ No depth here.

> I became interested in this when I realised that I wasn't going to get good enough grades to study to be a vet at university.

✗ Not a good admission to make.

> I have since noticed how much things like climate change are on the TV news.

✗ Not specific enough.

> I have always been interested in animals, and keep reptiles at home, and would like to learn more about them and how they behave.

✗ So does he still want to be a vet really?

> I am taking Biology and Geography A levels along with music because it is the other thing I am very interested in.
>   I play guitar for an indie rock band called Armageddon Death Bomb, which I started with some friends at school. We have worked really hard, and practice most days, which can make it difficult to keep up with school work. We are hoping to play at some festivals this summer and if we do well I might take a gap year to see if we can be successful.

✗ This shows commitment, but not to anything academic or relevant to the degree, and suggests that university is actually plan B if the music career doesn't take off.

> To keep fit I skateboard, and I use my board to get around which saves money and is a sustainable form of transport. I also like to go surfing, so am interested in studying at a university near the sea.

✗ Inappropriate as a main choice of university, although it might be one factor to consider. This is also very short – use the space provided.

TOP TIPS FOR A GOOD PERSONAL STATEMENT

1 In the opening paragraph, let the tutor know why it is that you have been drawn towards the subject and what evidence you can provide that indicates that you have an understanding of the demands of the course

2 Let them know about any extended reading or fieldwork opportunities that you might have had or any extracurricular interests that pertain to the degree specifically, for example conservation projects or recycling initiatives

3 Promote your existing skills in science-based subjects and other related subjects such as geography

4 Show that you are aware of the current issues that relate to the subject and that you read quality journalism and literature. Mention any particular area of the subject that particularly interests you and explain why

5 Give some indication that you are an independent learning with the personal initiative required to thrive in this environment

6 Tell us about your interests beyond school and college.

THINGS TO AVOID

1 Spelling and punctuation mistakes – get your statement proofread carefully

2 Lies or claims that you would struggle to defend in an interview

3 Copying someone else's statement – we want to get to know *you* not them!

4 Too much emphasis on interests that are irrelevant to your chosen course

5 Not using up the full amount of space – this leaves a bad impression unless the rest of the statement is outstanding.

RECOMMENDED READING AND WEBSITES

- CRAC Degree Course Guide: *Environmental Sciences*, Richmond: CRAC/ Trotman Publishing, 2006
- Works by authors such as Richard Dawkins, Steve Jones, James Lovelock, Aldo Leopold, Rachel Carson are good for general reading around the subject
- *New Scientist* (www.newscientist.com)
- Quality newspapers for environmental news stories or editorials
- I am grateful to the Environmental Science department at Southampton (www.civil.soton.ac.uk/es) for their support in compiling this profile.

FINE ART AND ART FOUNDATION

This academic profile was written using information provided by an admissions tutor from Dundee University (which includes the Duncan Jordanstone College). The information in this profile is useful to all applicants, but please be aware that some of the advice is pertinent to that department in particular.

SUBJECT OVERVIEW

Students wishing to study fine art at university normally undertake a one-year foundation programme first which equips them to apply for a three-year BA honours degree in Fine Art. In Scotland students enter a four-year degree programme in art or design, the first year of which is normally a diagnostic General Foundation in Art and Design.

The first aim of a foundation course is the development of your ability, skill and critical faculties by means of thoughtful study and visual outcomes. An awareness of the broad nature of art and design underlies the teaching of the course. The process of acquiring sound basic skills includes consideration of creativity, aesthetics, visual awareness, and analytical and critical faculties. Knowledge and a sense and understanding of the history, theory and practice of art and design is cultivated, allowing you to place yourself, your work and aspirations in context.

The second aim is to help you decide from the varied modules undertaken, your choice of degree study for the subsequent three years. The make-up of the modules has been carefully devised to enable you to gain a broad experience, awareness and skill level allied to art and design practices. Parallel to this is the contribution the overall dynamics of the course, as a learning experience, makes to the progressive development of your sense of connection to a specific area of subject specialism.

These twin aims are achieved through students working alongside each other in studios on projects led by academic staff.

During their foundation year students will apply to the degree specialism of their choice. This will involve preparing an application and accompanying portfolio. Students may be invited for an interview. The selection process will identify students who will benefit from a fine art education. The aims of a fine art programme include:

- To offer students the opportunity to develop their potential as independent artists in a multidisciplinary culture and an atmosphere of creative innovation and endeavour
- To produce graduates who are confident in their chosen areas of practice, who have developed visual imagination and awareness, and have acquired many personal and interpersonal, professional, transferable and research skills
- To develop the students' understanding of the artistic, historical, theoretical and cultural context which informs and shapes practice
- To develop the student's critical and self-critical capacities.

Students on fine art programmes may specialise in one particular discipline, such as sculpture, but increasingly students work across a range of visual disciplines in pursuit of the visualisation of their ideas. They will have opportunities to participate in study visits and to display their work in exhibitions. Most degree programmes will culminate in an annual public degree exhibition.

WHAT SKILLS OR ATTRIBUTES DO ADMISSIONS TUTORS LOOK FOR IN A GOOD APPLICANT?

Your portfolio will be considered to assess your enthusiasm, creativity, intellectual and practical skills in the practice of art and design. Consideration will be given to your potential for further development and progress in any of the fields of art and design the college has to offer.

The selector(s) will also be looking for indications of your visual awareness, the range of your interests and experience and the level of your commitment to art and design. Your portfolio should include representative examples of work undertaken as part of a programme of study. The compilation of a portfolio should not be regarded as an end in itself, but rather as one of the results of that study. It is the primary means by which you present yourself to the selector, so you should prepare it accordingly.

WHAT DOES A GOOD PERSONAL STATEMENT LOOK LIKE?

Your portfolio is the primary tool for the selection process, but your personal statement adds a valuable context. It should be imaginative and creative. You should demonstrate creativity and a desire to pursue a career in art. Admissions tutors are interested in hearing about school and extracurricular activities, but only where they demonstrate in a broader context how they have helped develop you as a person in relation to your artistic aspirations.

Examples from good personal statements

> **Having been involved in and thoroughly enjoyed art and design during my years at school, culminating in advanced Higher Art and Design and portfolio this year, I am now sure that my chosen future career will be art-related.**

✓ This is a clear, unambiguous and honest opening sentence.

It may seem unoriginal but the arts have always been an important part of my life. I would describe myself as a creative person and am interested in the links between the visual arts and language. To quote artist Jackson Pollock 'It is all a big game of construction – some with a brush, others choose a pen.'

✓ This opening shows a wider awareness of the cultural context of art. It also demonstrates an appreciation of the links between different aspects of creative arts.

Summer of 2006 enabled me to address my future and determine my choice of study. It was during that time that I realised that my interests in both art and computer graphics could be combined. I was very lucky to get the opportunity to work with a games company as a games tester. I gained invaluable experience in learning how the business side of the industry worked as well as the creative process.

During my fifth year at school I found the Higher Art course enjoyably challenging. I had to work to strict deadlines on two units – jewellery design producing a piece inspired by the Botanic Gardens, and portraiture, which involved painting a self-portrait. I also learned about several painters from different movements. During that year I also attended a summer school at a local college and went on to join a life drawing class and portfolio building class.

✓ These two examples demonstrate the initiative and commitment shown through a wider involvement with art-related studies beyond the school or FE curriculum.

Outside of college I have a part-time job in Asda where I interact with many different types of people, colleagues and customers. This job has helped me improve my communication skills in day to day life and to become more confident. At school I enjoyed the challenge of being the chair of a school committee which organised events to raise money for charity both in and outside school. For example, we raised funds for Red Nose Day and I was involved in making posters to raise awareness as well as making a short film which was shown to various year groups to encourage fellow pupils and staff to give money.

✓ An individual demonstrating how they invest their creative abilities in a wider context.

I was also a prefect, a role from which I learned better timekeeping and became more mature and responsible. I also developed other skills during my time in sixth year through helping a first year academically and socially as part of the buddying system. Not only did I enjoy this but I learned to listen and be patient and to be aware of how other people use situation.

✓ An acknowledgement of the collective responsibility and contribution that can be made in a community. It also displays an awareness of the personal attributes acquired through taking on roles of responsibility

I decided I wanted to study Art so I looked at various course options. I had heard that particular courses were excellent so I took the opportunity to go to their open days. I was particularly attracted by the course at. . . and the foundation year seemed a good way to discover which area of art would suit me, however at present I feel I would like to pursue sculpture.'

✓ Shows that the applicant has seriously researched the options available and made a considered choice of application.

The following statement stood out from the crowd – it was the second year that the student had applied and this statement played a strong supporting role to her portfolio in the decision to offer her a place. She is now studying graphic design.

Me? I love: unexpected snow, my friends, surprises, gifts, noodles, music, computing, socialising, writing, spontaneity, the smell of petrol/bleach/vanilla, strawberry jam, old photographs, my family, meddling, new socks, guitars, being random, driving through puddles, heavy rain, apple juice, gigs, camping, tartan mini skirts with hoodies and so much more, but above all else I love art. I know that may seem like one heck of a generalisation, but it's true. I love everything from paintings that seem like photographs (Michelangelo) to ones which verge on the obscure (Francis Bacon), sketches which must have taken hours (Da Vinci) to comic strips (John Allison), graffiti (Banksy) to elaborate sculptures (Mark Quinn) and everything in between!

This year I have been indulging and further extending my love for all things arty by attending Dundee College on a full-time portfolio course. Through this I feel that I have greatly enhanced my skills and knowledge in drawing, design and painting. In general I enjoy the expressive subjects more than design but on the whole I enjoy the whole course, with my favourite class changing every week! I also feel that my social and interpersonal skills have developed as I have made many new friends and had the chance to meet people who I otherwise would have not.

In particular my life drawing has come on tremendously. I currently attend a night course at college and am thoroughly enjoying it as I never had the chance to do it at school and I feel it helps, not just with my life drawing, but also other aspects of the subject. I also plan to start a night class on using Dreamweaver later in the year as I am particularly interested in the areas of graphic design and the internet.

Going to Dundee College has meant that I have had to give up my cleaning job as the hours were incompatible as I have to travel by train every day and I arrive home late at night but it's all been worthwhile.

Outside of college I enjoy going to various art galleries to look at what is happening in the art world and to see different exhibitions. I feel that it is important to have an interest in a wide variety of art as all aspects of it overlap and tie in with each other, so a technique used in fine art may in fact help with something in design. This way I feel that I am broadening the range of techniques and skills I have for the future.

Although the workload has been demanding this year I have found it a welcome change to school were I was vice captain of my house and had to perform various duties such as organising house events and maintaining the house noticeboard (a harder task than it sounds when you get no help from your captain!). I was also in charge of the lockers, which meant I had to make sure they were properly maintained and distributed. All the duties I had to perform in secondary school have helped make me become more organised and more reliable. I also now know that I am capable of working not just in a team but I can also work on my own competently.

Overall I feel that I am ready to further my education by attending university where I hope to continue to enjoy the subject as much as I have done in the past and to carry on learning and adding to my artistic abilities. I believe that I am a conscientious, organised and self-motivated person who will cope well with the demands of university life. Irrespective of my long-term career path, I am confident that my all-round abilities would serve me well in an art course. I am keen to broaden my horizons in an academic, social and personal sense and feel that university study will provide many opportunities for development.

Examples from poor personal statements

It was clear to me from a very young age that art was my great passion, not only because I was told I was talented, but because I enjoyed everything about it. I was never happier than when spending all my hours in the school art department.

✗ This opening paragraph is a cliché – both in language and sentiment.

As a child I was deeply unhappy if I didn't have my crayons with me. In my spare time I like to read, sketch or paint. I get a real thrill and am inspired by producing a completely original piece of work. This feeling drives me to achieve my ambition at a much higher level.

✗ This comes across as being naïve. It reads as if this is a hobby rather than a serious commitment.

I was elected school prefect in my final year and was involved in an anti-bullying initiative. I also attend a local church and teach in the Sunday School.

For several years I attended karate lessons. At present I am in my second year of being a prefect at school, which is a very responsible position. I study a lot in my free time as well as working part-time doing clerical work in a local office. In school I was asked by the learning support unit to assist students with learning difficulties with their school work.

✗ This is just a list of achievements with no acknowledgement of the skills they have developed through these activities.

 **TOP TIPS FOR A GOOD PERSONAL STATEMENT**

1 Your portfolio is the primary tool for the selection process, but your personal statement adds a valuable context – it should be imaginative and creative

2 Get someone else to read over your statement before you send it. It is very easy to overlook grammatical and spelling errors, lack of punctuation, repetition, and omitting vital information

3 Emphasise your love of art and the artistic process – convey this passion in a way that is compelling and unusual

4 Draw on what influences you now and any artist or artistic genre you find compelling.

 THINGS TO AVOID

1 Copying examples of personal statements you find on the web – you should only use them as a guideline. They are easy to spot and result in statements that do not show the individuality that selectors are looking for

2 Using clichés and overtly 'arty' language

3 Implying that art is a hobby, not an intellectual passion

4 Telling lies and near-truths that can be exposed at interview.

 RECOMMENDED READING AND WEBSITES

- Alan Pipes, *Foundations of Art and Design*, London: Laurence King Publishing, 2008
- James Burnett, *Getting Into Art and Design Courses*, Richmond: Trotman Publishing, 2008
- *Trotman's Green Guides: Art, Design and Performing Arts Courses*, Richmond: Trotman Publishing, annual
- *The Art & Design Directory*, Inspiring Futures Foundation, annual
- I am grateful for the support of Duncan Jordanstone College of Art & Design (www.djcad.dundee.ac.uk) in compiling this profile.

GEOGRAPHY

This academic profile was written using information provided by an admissions tutor at Royal Holloway, University of London. The information in this profile is useful to all applicants, but some of the advice is pertinent to that department in particular.

SUBJECT OVERVIEW

Geography is a diverse and exciting subject, which allows students to explore and understand the key environmental, economic, social and political challenges we face in the modern world.

Learning about the environment, sustainable development, climate change, globalisation and other issues that affect our lives is an essential part of modern geography. The subject is unique in providing a bridge between the social sciences, with their understanding of the dynamics of societies, cultures and behaviour, and the environmental sciences with their understanding of physical landscapes and the dynamics of environmental processes. The interaction between people and the environment lies at the heart of the discipline and is essential to contemporary understanding of today's global problems.

By studying such a broad subject, students obtain a range of learning experiences and skills that make geography graduates highly attractive to future employers.

The Royal Geographical Society advocates that on completion of your degree you will have many skills in preparation for work. These will be integral to your training, and to your employability, and should include:

Intellectual skills, such as critically evaluating theories and judging evidence to make informed decisions and to develop reasoned arguments.

Geography-specific skills, such as undertaking a piece of research, using a range of technical methods for the collection and analysis of spatial and environmental data, and undertaking fieldwork.

Key transferable skills in communication, presentation, debate numerical analysis, teamwork, problem solving, report and essay writing and many IT skills.

Personal attributes, such as time management, development of responsibility, coping with uncertainty, self-reflection, motivation, flexibility, and creativity.

WHAT SKILLS AND ATTRIBUTES DO ADMISSIONS TUTORS LOOK FOR IN A GOOD APPLICANT?

We are looking for individuals who are passionate about geography and curious about the world in which we live. It is important that this interest goes beyond the confines of the curriculum and classroom, for example through attending outside lectures or reading geography-related books or magazines. You should be able to see how geography helps explain human and environmental processes in their everyday lives.

Studying at university requires students to be self-motivated and independent. Applicants need to have developed good communication skills that allow them to present information effectively in both written and oral forms. They also need to have good ICT and data analysis skills. To manage their time successfully and to work in groups.

Good applicants are well-rounded individuals who have interests beyond their schoolwork. Activities such as sport, music and drama, as well as community work or paid employment, all involve skills development and will help you meet the challenges of university study.

WHAT DOES A GOOD PERSONAL STATEMENT LOOK LIKE?

Example from a good personal statement

From an applicant who wants to study a physical geography course.

I have always been fascinated with geography and the way in which landforms are created. I enjoy both physical and human geography, but my main interests lie in the physical aspects. Pursuing geography to degree level has been a logical step for me. I want to develop my knowledge of geomorphological and environmental processes and, after graduation, find employment in a related field in either an academic or commercial environment.

My school fieldtrip to Arran gave me the opportunity to investigate a very different landscape, and see the role of tectonic processes and glaciation in forming features such as sills and dykes, raised beaches and U-shaped valleys. I regularly attend Geographical Association lectures and particularly enjoyed a recent talk on coastal management in East Anglia. I also subscribe to 'Geography Review' magazine, which helps develop my understanding of geography.

My other A level subjects complement my interest in geography. For example, Biology has helped me when studying ecosystems and Maths has been important in the statistical analysis of fieldwork data. In all my A level courses, I have developed my skills in presenting information in written and oral form and using ICT.

For my work experience, I spent a week in the environmental department of the local council, focusing on their work-related to the sustainable management of rivers and floodplains. With the increasing demand for housing in my local area, it is vital that planners consider flood risk when making decisions about urban development. I attended community consultation meetings as well as analysing maps showing high-risk floodplain locations. Such work demonstrates the practical contributions that Geography can make in improving our lives.

I am passionate about sport and have played football for my school team for the past five years. Last year I was selected to play at county level and I hope to continue playing at university. Combining sport and schoolwork requires good time management and organisation. Outside of school time I have a part-time job at my local supermarket. This has improved my self-confidence, teamwork and communication skills.

I believe that I am a hard-working and motivated student, who can prioritise and deal with workloads and deadlines. I can use my initiative and remain open-minded. I believe that university will allow me to become even more independent and will provide many opportunities to broaden my interests further. The chance to increase my knowledge in a subject that I enjoy immensely is extremely attractive.

The key aspects that make this a good personal statement are:

- A strong opening statement that shows why the applicant wants to study geography.
- Evidence that they understand what geography is about and what they have learned from your study of geography so far. Bringing in some

details about the landforms of Arran helps support claims about being interested in landform formation.

- Including information about geography-related activities (going to Geographical Association lectures and reading *Geography Review*) demonstrates an interest and curiosity in the subject that goes beyond the classroom.
- An awareness of how geography intersects with other subjects and what skills they have developed in their A levels.
- Recognition of how geography can be applied to real-world problems. This shows that they have thought about what geography is as a subject.
- Information about interests and work experience, and what skills they have helped the applicant to develop.
- A final section summing up what personal qualities they have that make them suitable to study geography at university.
- No spelling or grammar mistakes.

TOP TIPS FOR A GOOD PERSONAL STATEMENT

1 Indicate that you understand what geography is about and that you are aware of the demands of the course

2 Show clearly any experience that you have of coursework and fieldwork and what they taught you

3 Indicate an awareness of how geography intersects with other subjects and what skills you have gained from the study of your other A levels

4 Provide evidence of your extra curricular pursuits, particularly where these indicate leadership potential or personal initiative.

THINGS TO AVOID

1 Poor spelling, punctuation and grammar

2 Underselling your current skills

3 Indicating a poor understanding of the demands of the course due to poor research – for instance, confusing physical and human geography.

RECOMMENDED READING AND WEBSITES

- Paul Cloke, Philip Crang and Mark Goodwin (eds), *Introducing Human Geographies*, 2nd edition, London: Hodder Arnold, 2005
- Peter Daniels, Michael Bradshaw, Denis Shaw and James Sidaway, *An Introduction to Human Geography: Issues for the 21st Century*, 3rd edition, London: Pearson, 2008
- Joseph Holden (ed) (2008) *An Introduction to Physical Geography and the Environment*, 2nd edition, London: Prentice Hall
- *Geography Review* magazine. Published four times a year by Philip Allan (www.philipallan.co.uk)
- The Royal Geographical Society with The Institute of British Geographers (www.rgs.org; http://studygeography.rgs.org)
- CRAC Degree Course Guide: *Geography and Geological Sciences*, Richmond: CRAC/Trotman Publishing, 2006
- I am grateful for the support of Royal Holloway (www.gg.rhul.ac.uk) in the compiling of this profile.

GEOLOGY

This academic profile was written an admissions tutor at Southampton University. The information in this profile is useful to all applicants, but some of the advice is pertinent to Southampton in particular.

SUBJECT OVERVIEW

An undergraduate degree in Geology will involve many diverse, but integrated activities: lectures to provide theory and knowledge, laboratory practicals to teach fundamental analytical and practical skills, and fieldwork, both on one-day excursions and residential courses in the UK and abroad, to provide hands-on training in geological field techniques and mapping.

To understand the nature, dynamics and evolution of the physical, chemical and biological processes operating on the Earth over the past four billion years, a course will integrate aspects of most of the physical sciences: chemistry, physics, maths, biology and geography, producing all-round science graduates. All good courses will include instruction and practice in professional key skills such as report/essay writing, giving lectures and presentations and presenting papers and posters, all things you will be doing as a graduate scientist. All of this information will be provided in a coherent and progressive manner, and there will be a huge variety of different assessment methods, from written and practical exams to teamwork projects, independent research, posters and oral presentations, all delivered in a way that is accessible and enjoyable to all. Being taught at a research-led university will ensure that your teaching is delivered by active researchers in their own field of expertise – always beneficial because research scientists can be counted on not only to be enthusiastic about their subject and to pass on their enthusiasm to you, but also to provide instruction on cutting-edge topics that form the current focus of international investigation.

A diverse variety of course modules are the key to a good Geology degree, and you should expect to be taught topics as diverse as bio molecular palaeontology and geological hazards, geochemistry and palaeoclimate change. You should expect to be challenged and have your abilities stretched throughout the duration of your degree, and be able to demonstrate that you can apply what you have learnt in problem-based exercises.

Fieldwork should be a key element, you should be taught how to use field equipment and how to collect, analyse and interpret a variety of different types of field data and samples. All degree courses accredited by The Geological Society of London will offer an independent mapping project of some form, taking the form of several weeks' worth of field surveying somewhere in the world, usually in the summer vacation between the second and third years of study. There will be support staff to guide and instruct you to successfully complete these specialised activities, but self-motivation and time management skills are also essential!

Most universities will provide opportunities for the most talented students to conduct a period of study abroad at a partner institution, and there will be many other opportunities for involvement in extracurricular or directly degree-related research activities to be incorporated into a geological degree. Above all, if you have a degree of independence, a great deal of drive and motivation for field-based activities, you will find a degree in Geology to be a hugely rewarding experience.

WHAT SKILLS OR ATTRIBUTES DO ADMISSIONS TUTORS LOOK FOR IN A GOOD APPLICANT?

Applicants should display a drive and enthusiasm for, and an informed understanding of the degree programme(s) for which they have applied, and should be able to demonstrate that they have thoroughly researched the subject area and have considered why they wish to undertake such a degree in the context of their future career development. Applicants will be expected to have ensured that their academic background and the examinations they are yet to secure are acceptable, and their qualifications will be of a sufficient level of attainment, to ensure admission to the course of their choice.

The applicants should provide sufficient information in their personal statement to indicate that they not only appreciate the personal skills and abilities required for successful completion of an earth science degree, but that they can illustrate such an appreciation with pertinent personal examples in the form of educationally-based experiences (for example, personal and team-based sporting or musical activities), extracurricular or work experiences. If an applicant can provide evidence or demonstrate well-developed time and personal management skills, English language, grammar and numerical skills, along with a degree of independence, these are all aspects of a candidate's character that will be of interest to admissions staff.

WHAT DOES A GOOD PERSONAL STATEMENT LOOK LIKE?

Your personal statement should provide an admissions tutor with sufficient information to convey that you have not only a drive and enthusiasm for the degree programme(s) for which you are applying, but also that you have thoroughly researched the subject area and have considered why you wish to undertake such a degree in the context of your future career development. As a potential applicant you will be expected to tailor your personal statement to address your interest in the wider subject discipline and perhaps in specific areas of the discipline. To realise this you may choose to draw upon your own experiences in AS/A2 level subjects, involvement in subject-related extracurricular activities or work experience. This part of the statement ought to comprise some 30–50% of the whole statement, and should be reflective and demonstrate self-awareness.

As all earth and marine science subject areas will have a practical, field-based component, you ought to highlight any such experience and skills which you already have, be it study-based (for example, A levels), or extracurricular (for example, Duke of Edinburgh's Award Scheme, Operation Raleigh, or activity-style holidays you have organised for yourself). However, many of the personal skills and abilities required for successful completion of an earth or marine science degree can also be demonstrated by reference to other forms of education-based experience (for example, personal and individual/team-based sporting or musical activities), or work experience. Avoid meaningless literary quotes or apparent deep thoughtful insights about your chosen topic that you have picked off a website or invented – admission tutors have read most of them already!

Example of a good personal statement

> While one child may have picked up a rock and skimmed it across the sea, my inquiring mind would not let me do this – I had to know more about it: where it came from, how it was formed. As a young child I was fascinated by rocks and earth materials around me – as I grew older, learning about plate tectonics and earthquakes through secondary school intrigued me further. I am currently studying Biology and Chemistry, both of which have a strong affiliation to Geology and have provided me with additional scientific skills

applicable to my Geography course. I came to understand more about igneous, sedimentary and metamorphic rocks, permeable and impermeable rocks and the properties of materials such as chalk and clay, and I have recently attended a Geography Masterclass at the University of X, where aspects of environmental geography were discussed and developed. I subscribe to 'Geology Today' in which I have read articles such as 'From microscopic minerals to global climate change' by David J Brown & Martin Lee. Articles of this kind have provided me with more in-depth geologists' views on the causes of climate change.

I have recently conducted fieldtrips to The Lizard in Cornwall, where one can stand up on the Moho, and up to the top of Mount Nephin in Ireland. It was in Ireland where I completed my pilot study, mapping a series of dykes inside a mainly metamorphic region. Earlier this year I went on fieldwork to Le Massif Central in France where I completed my coursework of mapping and deducing the geological history of the area around Lac Chambon, and it was in France that I finally realised the true scale to which I am amazed by volcanoes while stood at the top of Puie du Marie. On these trips I have gained valuable knowledge from the field and a first-hand understanding of Geology. I especially enjoy the challenge of fieldwork, as I get the chance to explore new regions and broaden my ever expanding horizons, making the most of what I can achieve: be it climbing a rock face to investigate a mineral vein, or contemplating a geological map. I'm a very 'outdoors' person and adverse weather doesn't bother me!

My desire to obtain a glimpse into what life is like as a geological researcher drove me to apply for a position on a five-week expedition to Disko Island, off the western coast of Greenland this summer. While in Greenland we studied how glaciers had formed the valleys there, and mapped some of the geological. The data we gathered about the movement of the snouts of glaciers will be accessible to scientists around the world for research into climate change. This expedition not only let me experience geological fieldwork but caused me to repeatedly reach my personal limits and push them even further, improving my motivation and determination, and allowing me to develop as a person. The expedition also required me to raise over £4,500 in under a year, which I achieved through working part-time, participating in a sponsored run and organising a first aid course for local mountaineers.

I have a fascination for the role played by geologists in the developing world, and the positive contribution of geologists to the crisis that we currently face as a global community is something that has inspired me very much. The scarcity of resources and the impact of global climate change are developments I find both worrying and fascinating, and I understand that there is particular demand for geologists who can make accurate decisions for governments and warn about natural hazards. However, my current plans are to work in the oil and gas mining industry, or possibly civil or environmental engineering.

I have been actively involved in several projects in school, which I believe have provided me with opportunities to mature as a young person. I am currently mentoring students in the year below me and helping them to achieve similar success. Last year, I became a reading partner for younger students, which I feel greatly benefited them as well as giving me valuable experience in working sympathetically with younger children. In my spare time I enjoy participating in sports, and am a qualified RYA Dinghy Instructor and later this year will be completing my Basic Expedition Leadership Award, which will allow me to run Duke of Edinburgh's Award expeditions. I also enjoy supporting others, and was a Prefect in the Lower Sixth and am currently on the Senior Prefect team at my school for the Upper Sixth. My voluntary teaching at my sailing club is recognised by the Millennium Volunteer scheme, where I have so far spent over 150 hours volunteering. These hobbies have developed my leadership skills and have pushed me to manage my time effectively, so that I can make the most of all the opportunities open to me. Furthermore, I have had the opportunity to meet a wide range of people and learn important skills in leadership and communication. I feel I have the maturity and enthusiasm to appreciate the academic opportunities offered at university and I am looking forward to participating in the activities that are available.

✓ This personal statement covers all of the subjects that admissions tutors in this subject area wish to read about. There is evidence of the candidate's enthusiasm for the degree subject for which they have applied, and the statement illustrates their in-depth understanding and appreciation of the specific areas of the discipline. The applicant provides ample indications of their drive and interest in the subject by having made strenuous efforts to accumulate subject-based practical extracurricular experience (although we do not expect all applicants to offer such 'exotic' experience!). In later parts of the statement the applicant indicates very strong self-awareness of their own skills, abilities and limitations – and their willingness to push themselves in every aspect of their life – both academic and personal – invaluable information for someone trying to assess an applicant's aptitude for university-level studies.

📝 TOP TIPS FOR A GOOD PERSONAL STATEMENT

1 Although this is not directly related to the statement, please ensure your qualifications meet published admissions criteria for the particular degree course for which you are applying (you'd be amazed at the number of applications that get rejected due to applicants applying without the correct subjects or number of qualifications)

THINGS TO AVOID

1 Applying for courses without having checked you have the correct qualifications to offer

2 Poor spelling and use of grammar

3 If you are applying for several different but related subjects on your UCAS form, do not focus your personal statement on one of these to the detriment of the others – admissions tutors only see the degree course you have applied for at their individual

2 Provide honest and reflective comments about why you wish to study at university and what you want to achieve, as well as checking that your grammar and spelling are correct!

3 Describe and evaluate as fully as possible what you gained from the coursework and fieldwork you have already completed as part of your school or college.

institution and they will not be impressed if your statement focuses on a different course at another institution

4 Trying to impress using literary quotes, or unlikely and apparently deeply thoughtful insights about your degree subject.

RECOMMENDED READING AND WEBSITES

- CRAC Degree Course Guide: *Geography and Geological Sciences*, Richmond: CRAC/Trotman Publishing, 2006
- Geologists' Association (www.geologists.org.uk)
- I am grateful to the Geology department at the University of Southampton (www.soes.soton.ac.uk) for their support in compiling this profile.

HISTORY

This academic profile was written using information provided by an admissions tutor at Royal Holloway, University of London. The information in this profile is useful to all applicants, but some of the advice is pertinent to that department in particular.

SUBJECT OVERVIEW

With global societies changing at a rapid pace, history has perhaps never been so relevant. The study of history concerns our understanding of what it was to be human in another place and at another time. Exploring what others have felt, thought, and done in the past, expands our self-awareness and our understanding of how we have come to be who we are both as individuals and as members of a wider society.

Studying history sharpens your insights into the functioning of past societies, helping you to formulate a more critical awareness of current day problems. In understanding past cultures, and learning to respect the reasoned views of others, students learn the values of tolerance and acceptance of diversity, which are essential today. Furthermore, curiosity informs all historical enquiries and studying history encourages the application of skills of analysis, argument and critical thinking, which are all highly valued in the modern employment market.

WHAT SKILLS AND ATTRIBUTES DO ADMISSIONS TUTORS LOOK FOR IN A GOOD APPLICANT?

Most of all, admissions tutors are looking for enthusiasm for history; you need to want to steep yourself in the subject for three years. We are particularly looking for candidates who show that their enthusiasm goes far beyond the confines of the curriculum, for example by attending lectures, visiting historical sites, and reading widely in history in their spare time. Equally, we don't want you only to be interested in history; indication of commitment to cultural, sporting, political, or charitable interests is a sign that you are a rounded individual, capable of managing your time and contributing to the community.

WHAT DOES A GOOD PERSONAL STATEMENT LOOK LIKE?
Example of a good personal statement

I have always been fascinated by history, and am enormously looking forward to the chance to devote myself to the study of different historical periods and problems at university. As part of my A2 studies this year, I have been studying England under the Tudors, a course that I have really enjoyed. I have increased my knowledge and understanding of this course in my own time by attending evening lectures by prominent historians like David Starkey. I have also taken the opportunity to read some recent books providing a broader context to my studies, and have particularly enjoyed 'Reformation: Europe's House Divided' by Diarmaid MacCulloch. My other area of particular historical interest is the Crusades, and I have recently been reading 'God's War: A New History of the Crusades', by Christopher Tyerman, which offers a provocative new interpretation of the Crusades. I have also pursued my interest in medieval history by visiting castles on a recent family holiday in Wales, though I am not sure that my younger sister shared my appreciation of the finer points of fortifications!

The other subjects I am studying for A2 level reinforce my interest in history. Sociology helps to provide models for human behaviour, and historians have successfully applied the theories of sociologists like Max Weber to their studies of modern societies. Studying Shakespeare's 'Richard II' for my A2 course in English has helped me understand the ideals of kingship that were current during the reign of Elizabeth I.

Outside my schoolwork, I enjoy acting, and recently took the lead role in a school production of 'West Side Story'. I have also been involved in my local branch of Amnesty International, co-ordinating letter-writing campaigns for political prisoners. Fitting in these activities alongside my crowded school schedule has been hard work, but has encouraged me to manage my time effectively. I believe that this balance of work and other activities demonstrates that I will be able to flourish at university.

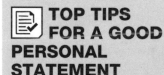

TOP TIPS FOR A GOOD PERSONAL STATEMENT

1 State clearly why you want to study history at university

2 Give evidence of real enthusiasm for the subject, which goes well beyond the confines of the curriculum

3 Draw appropriate connections between your chosen subject of History and your other subjects

4 Show that you have extracurricular interests, to indicate that you are a well-rounded individual who is able to balance various commitments and manage your time effectively.

THINGS TO AVOID

1 Spelling and punctuation errors

2 Lazy sentence construction and a lack of coherent structure and form

3 Lies about what you claim to have read and done

4 Plagiarism

5 Poor research in the first place, leading to poor decisions – this is often apparent in a statement that lacks evidence that you understand the course and its demands.

RECOMMENDED READING AND WEBSITES

- CRAC Degree Course Guide: *History, Archaeology and Politics*, Richmond: CRAC/Trotman Publishing, 2006
- *BBC History Magazine* (www.bbchistorymagazine.com)
- *History Today* (www.historytoday.com)
- I am grateful for the support given to me by the History department at Royal Holloway (www.rhul.ac.uk/history) in the production of this profile.

LAW AND CRIMINOLOGY

This profile has been written using a composite of information provided by a number of leading Law schools, including Birmingham University, Queen Mary's London and Bristol University Law School. The information is useful to all applicants but some details may be pertinent to those departments in particular.

SUBJECT OVERVIEW

The study of law is a varied and fascinating exercise. It is a course that studies the whole range of human activity, from birth to death including such diverse things as education, employment, marriage, family life, medicine, business, tax, compensation, crime, divorce and ultimately inheritance law. Contrary to the impression you might have from TV adverts and news items; law is not just about people suing their local council after falling over a badly sited bollard. Nor is it all high-profile libel cases involving well-known popular authors and politicians, or wigs, judges and the drama of the courtroom. Most lawyers in the UK work as individual solicitors or in small firms with a few partners. They service the needs of the local community and can be found in towns and cities throughout the UK. Some (fewer than 10%) work in large city firms and earn six-figure salaries. Most solicitors and barristers earn a good wage but far less than the minority of the city lawyers we hear about on the television!

A good law student will need to understand the law of contract, criminal law, land law, tort (civil wrongs such as libel), constitutional law, property law and more.

Another aspect of law is criminology, which is the study of crime and punishment: why people do it and what should happen to them. This is a separate course or can be studied with law as a joint honours course at some universities. The academic demands of criminology are less than single honours Law. Full details can be found if you access the UCAS course search facility.

A Law degree is about analysis, attention to detail, argument and communication. It's also about reading what are called primary sources: cases, Acts of Parliament, EU legislation, and so on. Law students are hardworking and generally the academic demands are high, with many of the top schools demanding grades at the top end of the academic spectrum. Offers of AAB and above are common in these schools. Some schools also demand the LNAT aptitude test.

WHAT SKILLS AND ATTRIBUTES DO ADMISSIONS TUTORS LOOK FOR IN A GOOD APPLICANT?

Most of all, admissions tutors are looking for enthusiasm for history; you need to want to steep yourself in the subject for three years. We are particularly looking for candidates who show that their enthusiasm goes far beyond the confines of the curriculum, for example by attending lectures, visiting historical sites, and reading widely in history in their spare time. Equally, we don't want you only to be interested in history; indication of commitment to cultural, sporting, political, or charitable interests is a sign that you are a rounded individual, capable of managing your time and contributing to the community.

Law students will thrive if they possess these skills, which are both academic and non-academic.

Good A level grades (particularly if you are applying to one of the popular schools). You will need grades of ABB or higher to apply successfully for these schools. Most do not accept General Studies or Critical Thinking as single A2 subjects, but do not discourage students from taking them. A GCSE pass in English and Maths (C or above) is commonly expected.

A willingness to read and evidence that you have read widely and written well, using information that you have read and digested. For that reason, studying A level or equivalent courses in History, English or Philosophy will serve you well. Discuss coursework or extended essays and the skills you have developed from that process of research and extended writing.

Law schools also look favourably on subjects that are academically rigorous such as maths, the core sciences, economics, geography, the ancient and modern languages and politics. Critical thinking skills are also well worth developing either via an exam or extra curricular reading. Membership of debating societies or evidence of quality student journalism is looked at positively.

Generally speaking, law schools do not expect students to know anything about academic law, so A level Law is not a prerequisite.

You can apply to Law with subjects that are not listed above, but if your profile lacks one or more of the above you will find it harder to be admitted.

Law students also tend to:

- Enjoy argument for its own sake (and like to win)
- Be genuinely interested in people
- Like the challenge of a really knotty problem
- Dislike waffle
- Like to see fairness and justice
- Incline towards logical thinking
- Pay good attention to detail
- Want to be able to master a detailed brief at short notice.

TOP TIPS FOR A GOOD PERSONAL STATEMENT

1 Write a compelling personal statement that sells your potential and current skills in a compelling and concise way. Law is mostly about the ability of the lawyer to write well. A good personal statement will tell a tutor a great deal about this latent ability

2 Get involved in extracurricular programmes, particularly those that involve working with people and requiring initiative and leadership. Mention these in your personal statement

3 Make sure that you are well informed by reading a good quality newspaper and taking an interest in the law and justice system so that you can mention this in your statement

4 Be yourself and promote clearly why you feel the law is the right move for you. Provide evidence where appropriate.

THINGS TO AVOID

1 A weak, poorly constructed personal statement that is further undermined by basic spelling and grammar errors

2 Emphasising that all you want to do is work in the top city law firm – most solicitors do not!

3 Plagiarism, lies and overinflated claims that may one day be held against you – lawyers are expected to be people with integrity!

RECOMMENDED READING AND WEBSITES

- CRAC Degree Course Guide: *Law and Accountancy,* (Richmond: CRAC/ Trotman Publishing, 2006
- Phil Harris, *An Introduction to Law*, Cambridge: Cambridge University Press, 2006

- Clare Rhoden and Simon Chesterman, *Studying Law at University: Everything You Need to Know*, Australia: Allen & Unwin, 2005
- I am grateful for the support of Birmingham University (www.bham.ac.uk), Queen Mary's London (www.qmul.ac.uk) and Bristol University Law School (www.bristol.ac.uk/law) in the production of this profile.

MARINE BIOLOGY

This academic profile was written by an admissions tutor at Southampton University. The information in this profile is useful to all applicants, but some of the advice is pertinent to Southampton in particular.

 ## SUBJECT OVERVIEW

Marine biology as an undergraduate degree is a subject that involves a lot of diverse, yet linked activities; lectures to provide theory and knowledge, laboratory practicals to teach fundamental analytical and taxonomic skills and fieldwork, both shore- and boat-based, to provide hands-on training in identification and survey abilities. To understand how marine animals and plants function, it is vital that any course also includes relevant aspects of marine chemistry, physics and geology; marine biology is one of the subsets of the science of oceanography and cannot be realistically studied in isolation.

All good courses will include instruction and practice in professional key skills such as report/essay writing, giving lectures and presentations and presenting papers and posters, all things you will be doing as a graduate scientist. All of this information should be provided in a coherent and progressive manner and in a way that is enjoyable to all. Being taught by active researchers is always a good sign, research scientists can be counted on to be enthusiastic about their subject and to pass on their enthusiasm to you.

Subject variety is the key to a good marine biology degree and you should expect to be taught topics as diverse as classic taxonomy and molecular ecology and as challenging as ocean physics and be able to apply what you have learnt. Fieldwork should be a key element, you should be taught how to use sampling equipment and instrument packages, then 'work up' the samples and data as well as how to plan and run a survey. Being able to scuba dive or drive boats isn't an essential element of a marine biology degree (most of the marine environment is a lot deeper than you can realistically dive and work and there will be support staff who specialise in these activities) but check that you can learn these skills recreationally if you wish to do so.

WHAT SKILLS OR ATTRIBUTES DO ADMISSIONS TUTORS LOOK FOR IN A GOOD APPLICANT?

You should display a drive and enthusiasm for, and an informed understanding of, the degree programme(s) for which you have applied, and should be able to demonstrate that you have thoroughly researched the subject area and have considered why you wish to undertake such a degree in the context of your future career development. Ensure that your academic background and the examinations you are yet to secure are acceptable, and that your qualifications will be of a sufficient level of attainment to ensure admission to the course of your choice.

You should provide sufficient information in their personal statement to indicate that you appreciate the personal skills and abilities required for successful completion of an earth science degree and should illustrate such an appreciation with pertinent personal examples in the form of education-based experiences (for example, personal and individual/team-based sporting or musical activities), extracurricular (for example, travel, Duke of Edinburgh's Award) or work experiences. If you can provide evidence or demonstrate well-developed time and personal management skills, English language, grammar and numerical skills, along with a degree of independence, these are all aspects of your character that will be of interest to admissions staff.

WHAT DOES A GOOD PERSONAL STATEMENT LOOK LIKE?

Example of a good personal statement

My aim is to study at university, with a view of doing further study in marine conservation. The reason for this choice is my interest in animals and the environment and the challenges that lie with them. I would like to work abroad in marine conservation, and I believe that this course would open many doors for me. I have a great fascination of the world and environment and am always interested in learning about it.

For my work experience I am currently a volunteer for the Sea Trust charity, assisting them with their cetacean surveys in the Irish Sea. This involves recording any sightings of cetaceans and then comparing relevant data to monitor change within the area. I intend to continue working with them and develop my skills so that I can take part in many more surveys and eventually large research trips. I have also done two weeks work experience at a veterinary surgery, which has allowed me to experience a different working environment, leaving me with the conclusion that animals need to be incorporated in my future career.

I have a great interest in animals and have been a volunteer at the XYZ animal sanctuary for 18 months, as well as a Pets as Therapy Junior visitor which allows me to gain experience of a variety of situations and contribute to the local community. I dog train at both open and championship level. I also achieved my GCDS Gold award.

I participated in The Young Enterprise Scheme, and was Managing Director of our company, Markone, taking us to the final where I was awarded best individual performance. I have developed many leadership skills and have learnt how to manage large teams of people and how to listen and ensure that operations run smoothly.

Sport plays a key part in my life. At school I am captain of the netball, rounders and hockey teams and am a Sports Leader, coaching many teams within the school. Outside of school I am a member of XYZ triathlon club and am a keen watersports enthusiast. I hold RYA Level 4 sailing and Level 2 windsurfing certificates and hope to qualify as a sailing instructor in the forthcoming months.

At school, I am currently Head Girl and fully embrace every moment I have. I am on both the Eco Schools and charity committees, taking part in many events, which has given me fantastic social and public speaking skills that I will be able to use in future life. I have achieved both Bronze and Silver Duke of Edinburgh's Award and am currently completing my Gold.

I believe that with my skills and passion for learning, I will be able to commit to this course, and fulfil my time at university.

TOP TIPS FOR A GOOD PERSONAL STATEMENT

1 Before starting to write your personal statement, ensure your qualifications meet published admissions criteria for the particular degree course for which you are applying

2 Provide honest and reflective comments about why you wish to study at university and what you want to achieve in your personal statement, as well as checking that your grammar and spelling are correct!

3 Your personal statement can be used to decide whether to take you if you drop a grade in your exams

4 Emphasise the skills that you already have and mention in particular the skills that you have developed that are pertinent

5 Mention your coursework (and if relevant, fieldwork) projects as these will more than likely be specific subjects of conversation during the interview

6 Make sure that you re read your statement before any interview, as this will certainly be used to generate questions. This is where lies and half-truths are exposed!

THINGS TO AVOID

1 If you are applying for several different but related subjects on your UCAS Form, do not focus your personal statement on one of these to the detriment of the others – admissions tutors only see the degree course you have applied for at their individual institution and they will not be impressed if your statement focuses on a different course at another institution.

2 Poor spelling and use of grammar

3 Lying or copying another person's statement

4 Trying to impress by using literary quotes, or unlikely and apparently deeply thoughtful insights about your degree subject.

RECOMMENDED READING AND WEBSITES

- CRAC Degree Course Guide: *Biological Sciences*, Richmond: CRAC/ Trotman Publishing, 2006
- *New Scientist* (www.newscientist.com)
- *Discover* (www.discovermagazine.com)
- *National Geographic* (www.nationalgeographic.com)
- *Nature* (www.nature.com)
- Royal Geographical Society (www.rgs.org)
- Geological Association (www.geologists.org.uk)
- I am grateful to the Marine Biology department at Southampton University (www.soton.ac.uk) for their assistance in compiling this profile.

MATHEMATICS

This academic profile was written by an admissions tutor at Royal Holloway, University of London. The information in this profile is useful to all applicants, but some of the advice is pertinent to that department in particular.

SUBJECT OVERVIEW

For some, mathematics is a pure science to be studied for its intrinsic beauty and logical structure. For many it means problem solving and the satisfaction of getting what is indisputably the 'right' answer. Others will consider the myriad and diverse applications of mathematics, in areas such as finance or quantum information. The truth is that mathematics encompasses all these and more, because each perspective is fundamentally linked to the others.

By studying mathematics you gain a diverse range of transferable skills, including how to apply a universal language in a multiplicity of situations and see connections between them. Mathematics also provides an excellent foundation for a variety of fulfilling career paths or opportunities for further study.

Every mathematician needs a basic toolkit of mathematical methods (like the basic algebra and calculus at A level) which are developed further at university, but the way you build on this foundation depends on your interests. The choices at Royal Holloway are numerous. You can choose to study pure mathematics in more depth: the structures of algebra, the rigorous foundation for the limiting processes of calculus, or the theory of numbers. You can learn about mathematical modelling – translating real-life problems into mathematical equations, and then solving those equations, for example in fluid dynamics, special relativity, or quantum mechanics. Other areas of study include discrete mathematics, statistics, cryptography, operational research and financial mathematics.

The ability to formulate problems logically, and then solve them accurately and incisively, is invaluable in many areas of life. A degree in Mathematics will equip you with many skills, including:

- Problem solving
- Logical thought processes
- Problem formulation
- Information gathering and analysis
- Spatial understanding
- Personal organisation
- Spoken and written communication
- Being able to understand and handle mathematical expressions confidently.

WHAT SKILLS AND ATTRIBUTES DO ADMISSIONS TUTORS LOOK FOR IN A GOOD APPLICANT?

The three things that interest us most are:

- Mathematics
- Mathematics
- Mathematics!

That is perhaps an oversimplification, but your mathematical talent is by far the most important factor for admissions tutors. Of course they are also looking for an enthusiasm that will sustain you over three or four years. University study is more independent than at school, so that time management skills, determination to succeed, and a good work ethic are also highly relevant. Evidence of social activities undertaken in your spare time is also useful.

WHAT DOES A GOOD PERSONAL STATEMENT LOOK LIKE?

A good personal statement is, above all, personal. It gives you the chance to speak directly to the admissions tutor about yourself, your reasons for choosing a particular degree programme, your choice of A level subjects, your personal interests and out-of-school activities, in summary what makes you tick.

Be honest: if you say that a particular branch of mathematics interests you, or you have read a particular book, then this is likely to be a topic of discussion at interview. Talk about your current skills and attributes, particularly if they are either mathematical (you might like puzzles, chess, strategy games) or non-academic (such as leadership, initiative or examples of personal challenges that you have overcome). Include anything that you would like the admissions tutor to know about you that would not be covered elsewhere on the form.

TOP TIPS FOR A GOOD PERSONAL STATEMENT

1 Your statement should be clear, concise and free from errors

2 Your statement should explain clearly in the opening paragraph why maths is you choice of degree and more importantly what evidence you can provide that supports this view

THINGS TO AVOID

1 Spelling and other mistakes

2 Poorly constructed sentences that do not follow logically

3 Underemphasising your skills and why they will be suitable for maths

4 Not mentioning your work ethic and attitude to individual learning

3 Mention it if you have obtained high scores in tests or taken part in national maths challenges

4 Mention your non-academic attributes, too – leadership, personal success in tasks and any work experience or taster courses

5 If you have a career in mind that lends itself to maths, let us know.

5 Appearing to be unsociable and unwilling to engage in extracurricular pursuits.

RECOMMENDED READING AND WEBSITES

- Tom Körner, *The Pleasures of Counting*, Cambridge: Cambridge University Press, 1996. This uses examples as diverse as the outbreak of cholera in Victorian Soho, the Battle of the Atlantic, African Eve, and the design of anchors to show the kind of problems that interest mathematicians and the kind of ways in which they attack them
- I am grateful for the support I received from the Maths department at Royal Holloway (www.ma.rhul.ac.uk) in the preparation of this profile.

MEDICINE

This academic profile was written an admissions tutor at Brighton and Sussex Medical School. The information is useful to all applicants, but some of the advice is pertinent to BSMS in particular.

UCAS permits you to apply to a maximum of four medical schools. Given the competition for places, it is imperative that you use all of your application slots. I recommend that you also apply for an alternative course in your fifth slot, with biomedical science, biochemistry and neuroscience being ideal alternatives. This way you may, should you gain a good degree, be able to enter medical school via one of the popular graduate entry schemes. Applicants without the required academic profile may find it possible to gain entry to one of the foundation courses, where a student is admitted to medical school after they complete a foundation year.

SUBJECT OVERVIEW

Becoming a doctor isn't an easy option – it takes years of study and hard work. As you learn the skills you need, you will also learn a great deal about yourself. If you like helping people there are few more rewarding or respected careers. You'll be part of a team of professionals and non-medical staff delivering care to the highest standards in the NHS. Medicine is about helping people – treating illness, providing advice and reassurance, and seeing the effects of both ill health and good health from the patient's point of view. You have to examine the symptoms presented by a patient, and consider a range of possible diagnoses of their cause. You must test your diagnosis, decide on the best course of treatment, and monitor progress. This demands an enquiring mind, the capacity to acquire and maintain high levels of knowledge that have to be constantly up to date, and the ability to relate to people as individuals each with their own health needs.

If you have that passion to improve people's lives and the determination to reach the highest standards, you will have many career opportunities. You can follow a path to one of many specialties, from working in a hospital as a surgeon to being based in the community as a GP. The training and support available to you in the NHS can help you get to the very top of your chosen career.

Medicine is a demanding profession, but one that repays the hard work and dedication it involves through the rich variety of career opportunities it offers. Whether helping patients, managing a hospital or pushing back the borders of medical research, you will have the satisfaction of knowing that you are making a positive contribution to society.

At university, you will be kept busy with a mixture of seminars, lectures, anatomy classes, clinical skills practice and patient interaction, depending on where you study. In later years you will spend more time with medical teams than in the classroom. Assessments may be through exams, written portfolios or practical tests. Medical students are also known for their busy social lives!

WHAT SKILLS OR ATTRIBUTES DO ADMISSIONS TUTORS LOOK FOR IN A GOOD APPLICANT?

You will need the ability, the commitment and the personal qualities necessary to become an excellent doctor. Academically, BSMS requires 340 UCAS points at A level, including an A in Biology or Chemistry at AS level. Many equivalent qualifications are accepted, depending on whether you have studied abroad, or already completed a degree. Most medical schools also require you to take the UK Clinical Aptitude (UKCAT: www.ukcat.co.uk) or Biomedical Admissions Test (BMAT: www.bmat.org.uk) test.

Just as important are a realistic attitude to medical training and clinical practice, a commitment to caring for others, the ability to communicate and work effectively within a team and to appreciate other people's point of view, and a willingness to accept responsibility.

WHAT DOES A GOOD PERSONAL STATEMENT LOOK LIKE?

Medicine is a diverse profession with specialties that suit a wide range of people. We want our student body to reflect the variety of the profession and of society as a whole, and are not looking for any one model of personal statement.

Your personal statement should contain a short introduction about why you want to study medicine. Indicate what relevant experience you have, perhaps with a GP, in a hospital, hospice, care home or with disabled groups, and how you have reflected on and learned from it. This work experience is hard to achieve but the fact that you have will tell us that you have the drive and passion to succeed.

Do let us know what you learnt from the work experience rather than just telling us what you did. The tutor will be looking for evidence that you know what it is like to be a doctor and know a bit about healthcare delivery. We need to weed out those who think it is like *ER* or *Holby City*!

Demonstrate your understanding of scientific and medical issues; regular reading will help. I suggest that you read quite widely, particularly in the lead up to your interview. You ought to be aware of issues in medicine that you will have heard discussed in broadsheet newspapers and scientific journals.

Include not only what you have learned through study but your other activities and non-academic achievements – sports, hobbies, travel, awards and so on. Show what relevant qualities you have developed from your experiences, for example in communicating, leadership or teamwork.

Avoid poor spelling, grammar and punctuation. This leaves a poor impression and while not hugely significant, you cannot really afford to be seen as careless when competition is so fierce.

TOP TIPS FOR A GOOD PERSONAL STATEMENT

1 Find out as much as you can about what it is like to be a doctor. Talk to healthcare professionals, read as much as you can and get some relevant work experience. Mention what you have learnt as a result in the statement and be willing to discuss it at interview

THINGS TO AVOID

1 Making any claims in your personal statement that you cannot substantiate at interview

2 Plagiarising any part of your personal statement – when admissions tutors read through over 2,000 applications, this soon becomes obvious

3 Taking an inflexible stance on contentious issues – you need to

2 Research the prospectuses and websites of a variety of medical schools, and visit some to make sure you find the course, teaching styles, facilities and location that are right for you. When you start your statement, it might be worth mentioning the fact that you have done this and the choices you have made reflect your interests and learning styles

3 Begin work on your personal statement early – the UCAS deadline for medicine courses is earlier than for other university programmes. Get comments from other people and write several drafts. Make sure you are happy with it before you submit it to UCAS

4 Read the BMA's excellent guide *Becoming a Doctor*, which you can download at the BMA website www.bma.org.uk. The advice there will help you construct a good statement and prepare for the interview.

be able to work with people who hold all kinds of opinions

4 Memorising set answers to the interview questions you think you might get – the interviewers will be able to get to know you better through a natural conversation

5 Going into medicine because other people want you to – don't succumb to their pressure if you don't feel it's the right choice for you.

 # RECOMMENDED READING AND WEBSITES

- CRAC Degree Course Guide: *Medical and Related Professions*, Richmond: CRAC/Trotman Publishing, 2006
- *Becoming a Doctor*, BMA website (www.bma.org.uk)
- General Medical Council (www.gmc-uk.org)
- *Tomorrow's Doctors* on the GMC website (www.gmc-uk.org/education/ undergraduate/undergraduate_policy/tomorrows_doctors.asp)
- I am grateful to the Brighton and Sussex Medical School (www.bsms.ac.uk) for their help in preparing this profile.

MIDWIFERY

This academic profile was written an admissions tutor at Swansea University. The information in this profile is useful to all applicants, but some of the advice is pertinent to Swansea in particular.

SUBJECT OVERVIEW

Midwives offer individual care to women and their families and help them take part in their own care planning during pregnancy. Both during and after pregnancy you will be with the new mother in her own locality.

Midwifery is as much about supporting the new mother and her partner, as helping with the birth of the baby. Support continues from the confirmation of the pregnancy through to the postnatal days after the baby is born.

The philosophy of a degree course in midwifery is to prepare a midwife who is able to practice at the point of registration. It is designed to build upon an individual's strengths and to value her life experiences to develop into a professional and motivated practitioner. Students develop a heightened level of self-awareness and sensitivity towards women and families throughout the programme.

The learner is expected to grow in confidence and self-awareness; to take responsibility for their personal and professional development. Students then emerge into the practice arena as lifelong learners – confident, competent and accountable for their own practice as a midwife meeting the challenges of contemporary practice.

WHAT SKILLS OR ATTRIBUTES DO ADMISSIONS TUTORS LOOK FOR IN A GOOD APPLICANT?

Candidates need to be caring and understanding individuals with a sensitive nature. Good communication skills are essential in this career.

Most candidates in the UK who wish to enter the degree programme at Swansea, must have achieved three A levels at grade C or above (2 AS levels = 1 A level), or a score of 240 tariff points (or equivalent), plus English/ Welsh language, Maths and a science at GCSE grade C or above. All students must be able to demonstrate key skills and numeracy. These requirements will vary between institutions.

Departments across the UK welcome applications from students of all ages including mature students who have evidence of recent appropriate study (within the last five years) and with alternative qualifications such as Access to higher education programmes.

The university treats all applications for admission on their individual merits and welcomes applications from candidates with a range of qualifications.

Many departments, including Swansea, due to the competition for a small number of places, cannot consider applications for deferred entry.

WHAT DOES A GOOD PERSONAL STATEMENT LOOK LIKE?

You should write convincingly about your clear understanding of the role of the midwife and how your experience and attributes fit well with a career in midwifery. You should research demands of the role and current NHS practice so that you can demonstrate your awareness of the role in the opening part of the statement, and show that you understand that midwives work with people from all walks of like and often in stressful situations. This may, but does not have to, involve some work experience or personal contact with a practising midwife.

We like to see evidence of the key skills required, both academic and non-academic, and would like to hear what particular skills you have developed in your A level or equivalent studies. The sciences are important to emphasise but we do also look for breadth – make sure that you know the academic demands of each department you apply to before writing your statement. We also look for clarity, good spelling and grammar and evidence that you are involved in a wide range of extracurricular pursuits.

TOP TIPS FOR A GOOD PERSONAL STATEMENT

1 Do all that you can to access information to lead you to really understand the rigours of a career in midwifery and the demands of a three-year midwifery degree

2 Be prepared to explain all of this in your statement and in the interview

3 Show us that you have the academic potential to cope with the demands of the subject, by alluding to these skills in your statement.

THINGS TO AVOID

1 Referring too much to your own birth experiences (if you have any)

2 Applying to become a midwife if your real interest lies in caring for babies and children

3 Spelling, punctuation and grammar mistakes – make sure that your statement is read carefully by another person before you submit it. Check that the spell check is set to UK as default.

RECOMMENDED READING AND WEBSITES

- *Careers Uncovered: Nursing and Midwifery:* Richmond: Trotman Publishing, 2006
- Penny Armstrong and Sheryl Fieldman, *A Midwife's Story*, London: Pinter & Martin, 2006
- Stella McKay Moffat and Pamela Lee, *A Pocket Guide for Student Midwives*, Oxford: Wiley Blackwell, 2006
- The Nursing and Midwifery Council (www.nmc-uk.org)

- Royal College of Nursing (www.rcn.org.uk)
- I am grateful to the Midwifery department at Swansea University (www.swan.ac.uk/ugcourses/HealthScience/BMidMidwifery) for their support in preparing this profile.

MODERN LANGUAGES

This academic profile was written with the help of the universities of Surrey and Birmingham. The information is useful to all applicants, but some of the advice is pertinent to those departments in particular.

SUBJECT OVERVIEW

Modern language courses in the UK tend towards the languages that are studied in most UK schools, namely French, German, Spanish and Italian. They can be studied as a single subject or as part of a joint honours degree. Popular combinations include modern languages with business, politics, economics, media studies, law and history. Other languages on offer in UK universities include Russian, Arabic, Hebrew, Mandarin, Japanese, Portuguese, Greek (modern) and the Nordic languages.

If you study single honours you will concentrate on one subject for all four years. In your first two years you will also often take one module chosen from a wide range across the university, but apart from that your studies will be devoted to a single subject. For combinations of two languages, you would normally apply to read a BA in Modern Languages. In joint honours programmes you will study one modern language equally weighted with another subject that is not a modern language.

Spending a year abroad is a common element of language courses. This can be extremely beneficial, as immersing yourself in a language as a resident of that country extends your knowledge significantly. This option is not cheap so bear that in mind when you apply.

WHAT SKILLS OR ATTRIBUTES DO ADMISSIONS TUTORS LOOK FOR IN A GOOD APPLICANT?

Usually the entry requirements are largely self-evident, in that you need a language to A level (or equivalent), but some courses allow you to start a language from the beginning. In fact, you can do pretty much all the languages from beginner level (sometimes called *ab initio*) – apart from French at Birmingham – but only in particular combinations.

For instance, if you're doing two modern languages you need to have one to A level, but you could start the other from beginner level. This is a common feature of many courses in the UK. For example, you might have German to A level, but you want to pick up Italian or Portuguese from scratch. You obviously wouldn't be able to start a single honours language course such as German studies from beginner level, though. You would need an A level in that language. It is distinctions like these that are important to note, and it shows why the research in advance is so vital. Every year about 5% of our applicants apply for courses for which they don't have the requisite qualifications and waste a choice on their UCAS forms. In a lot of cases it's because they have not done enough research before they complete their UCAS form.

Non-academic traits include a sound mind, an evident zest for life and an interest in languages and cultures. We need to see some evidence of this when we read a personal statement or interview a candidate.

WHAT DOES A GOOD PERSONAL STATEMENT LOOK LIKE?

Over the past four to five years, school teachers have become more aware that it is increasingly competitive, and they need to give more help and support to applicants with getting their personal statements right. What this seems to have done is create quite a number of 'template' personal statements that all look very much like each other. One of the things I recommend is to go for something a little different, without being idiosyncratic. Punctuation and grammar are also vital, especially if the course is competitive. If you say you're interested in languages, we want to know *why* you're interested in the course. What sparked that interest? What have you done to show that interest in a real way? For example, if you've been doing extra reading around the A level curriculum, write it down. Refer to books or magazines that you have read or read in the native language. Mention foreign travel, exchanges that you have been on or any other pertinent information that supports your case. If you are already bilingual, say so. It will give us an indication that you have a talent for languages, even if the languages that you speak are not those that you hope to read.

We're also looking for applicants who are likely to adapt to the university way of thinking. We're looking for a critical mindset, students who will be enquiring and analytical, and willing to get involved in intellectual debate. I like those who can convey that sense of excitement at getting involved in an intellectual debate.

Example of a good personal statement

> My decision to study French and Spanish stems not only from a genuine desire to further my knowledge, but also because of the experiences I have already had through using foreign languages.

✓ Relates past positive reactions of language-learning to future chosen course of study.

> I have chosen to study French because I am passionate about language learning. In my French studies I particular enjoy learning about French culture. One topic I found particularly interesting was 'Immigration and Multiculturalism' and how successfully North African immigrants, for instance, are integrated into French society.

✓ Shows openness to other cultures, multicultural perspectives.

> Through studying Spanish at A level I have learnt a great deal about the history of Spain, with topics such as the Spanish Civil War and the reign of Franco. I am also fascinated by Spanish culture and have learnt about the architecture of Gaudi and the art of the Flamenco.

✓ i.e awareness of how political and cultural influences shape language study

> During my German studies I went on a 5-day trip to Strasbourg, Freiburg and Baden Baden. A visit to the European Parliament – where the best interpreters and translators work – has given me a good insight into what an interpreter's career entails.

✓ Concrete evidence of unearthing vocational applications of languages.

TOP TIPS FOR A GOOD PERSONAL STATEMENT

1 Think hard about what you want to do before you start to write your personal statement

2 Think about what you enjoy and what you love and express this in your statement

3 If you are applying for a language, we need to know that you have the aptitude to succeed. Mention in your statement your current level of fluency, the experience you have of speaking the language with native speakers and any exchange trip you may have been involved with

4 Make sure that you personal statement is clear, concise, free from basic errors and sells yourself in a compelling manner.

THINGS TO AVOID

1 Lying on your personal statement – lies are often found out and this can lead to the reject bin or worse!

2 Plagiarising from another statement – be inspired by exemplars but ultimately be yourself! UCAS checks personal statements for signs of plagiarism and informs that university if they are suspicious

3 Spelling, punctuation and grammar errors on your statement – this is just lazy

4 Applying before you have done the right research – check the entry requirements and make sure that the course on offer plays to your strengths

5 Glib, generalised comments – they often irritate. It is a professional document and the language should be professional in tone, not too conversational or text-speak like!

RECOMMENDED READING AND WEBSITES

■ CRAC Degree Course Guide: *Modern Languages & European Studies*, Richmond: CRAC/Trotman Publishing, 2006

■ You should also read a range of different publications in the language you wish to study – newspapers, magazines (both serious and glossy), books and even comic books

■ I would like to acknowledge the support of the University of Surrey (www.surrey.ac.uk) and the University of Birmingham (www.bham.ac.uk) in producing this profile.

MUSIC

This academic profile was written by admissions tutors at Southampton University. The information is useful to all applicants, but some of the advice is pertinent to that department in particular.

At this point I would like to point out that you could also, if you think it is appropriate for you, apply to read music at one of the conservatoires. These are specialist music colleges with a strong emphasis on musical performance, conducting and composition. A very high level of musical aptitude is expected. Applications are made direct to the conservatoire or via the CUKAS system. (See Chapter Ten)

SUBJECT OVERVIEW

Studying music at university is like Christmas coming early all the year round. Everyone who contemplates a music degree will have been bitten by the music bug from an early age, and will have been spending most of their free time at school developing instrumental and vocal skills, learning about music and how to write it, and participating in ensembles from garage bands to symphony orchestras. At university, you get to continue this passion, except that you get to do it full time. There is no subject on offer at university with such a clear match between reality and your ambitions.

From your first day at university, you'll be engaged in understanding how music works and translating that understanding into the performances you want to give. You'll be taught by experts in your field and given lots of opportunities to display your knowledge in public performances in front of your peers and the rest of the community.

Career prospects for music graduates are excellent, since they are equipped with the crucial qualities of communication and self-expression, interaction and teamwork, and time management. Our graduates go on to careers in teaching, media, arts administration, performance, composition, journalism, production and sound engineering, and postgraduate study.

WHAT SKILLS OR ATTRIBUTES DO ADMISSIONS TUTORS LOOK FOR IN A GOOD APPLICANT?

We look for applicants with excellent A level results and with experience and abilities outside their A level curriculum. But a good applicant will also have a sustained profile in instrumental and vocal performance (any style or genre) with evidence of an ability to perform in public both as a soloist and as an ensemble player. This means you have to be an extrovert soloist but at the same time a team player able to work with your colleagues.

WHAT DOES A GOOD PERSONAL STATEMENT LOOK LIKE?

Be specific about your skills and experiences. What instruments do you play and to what level? Who have you studied with? What ensembles are you part of, and how long have you been a member? How does the practical work tie in with your A level academic work? Give clear indications as why you have chosen this type of institution for your degree, and make clear that you understand how these programmes match your ambitions. What do you do outside of music? In addition, the usual advice applies. Make sure that it is concise, precise and sells you skills well. Avoid spelling and punctuation errors and do not attempt to plagiarise material. This is both fraudulent and easily spotted at interview.

 ## TOP TIPS FOR A GOOD PERSONAL STATEMENT

1 Show us that you have made a personal investment in music beyond school and make this clear in the body of your personal statement

2 Convince us that you have a genuine interest in

THINGS TO AVOID

1 Being a specialist who only plays and listens to one kind of music – you need to be receptive to many musical styles and approaches to studying music to succeed in a music degree

2 A statement that is poorly written in terms of style and design. It should be treated as a

understanding music, and not just listening to it or performing it

3 Find out about the specific content of each university's course, and think carefully about which one best matches your interest: a candidate who has taken the trouble to research what we offer and is really enthused by it will come across well. This research will be evident in your statement

4 Approach us with a real understanding of what it is like to study music at university, and show us how your experiences so far have prepared you for or encouraged you towards a Music degree

5 Don't play down your other strengths and interests: we're looking for students who excel not just in music, but have performed well across their school curriculum. Ideally, give some thought to how your study of maths or English or media or whatever has enhanced your appreciation of music!

very important document and be given the time and effort that it deserves

3 Writing what you think we want to hear if it is not you. The **real** you will study at university and a false impression given in the statement will only hinder you in the long term

RECOMMENDED READING AND WEBSITES

- CRAC Degree Course Guide: *Music, Drama and Dance,* Richmond; CRAC/Trotman Publishing, 2007
- I am grateful to the Music department at Southampton (www.soton.ac.uk/music), for their assistance in writing this profile.

NURSING

This academic profile was written by admissions tutors at Swansea University. The information in this profile is useful to all applicants, but some of the advice is pertinent to that department in particular.

SUBJECT OVERVIEW

Nursing is a unique occupation and offers you a chance to help others when they need it most. There has never been a more exciting time to join the nursing profession. Nurses are crucial members of the multiprofessional healthcare team. The number and variety of nursing roles is extensive. Once qualified as a registered nurse, you will have opportunities to work in a range of environments including NHS and independent hospitals, GP surgeries, clinics, nursing and residential homes, occupational health services, voluntary organisations, armed forces and industry. Today there are greater opportunities for nurses to take increased responsibility for patient care and to become specialists and advanced practitioners in many areas, for example, intensive care, cancer care and mental health.

WHAT SKILLS OR ATTRIBUTES DO ADMISSIONS TUTORS LOOK FOR IN A GOOD APPLICANT?

You need the desire to help people. You have to be a practical individual and know how to manage your time. You will, as a nurse, develop effective communication skills and the ability to work in a team, but also act as a leader.

You need to demonstrate a strong educational profile and a clear commitment to your chosen branch of nursing. GCSE profile needs to include Welsh/English language, Maths and a science grade A–C. Entrance requirements vary from department to department. Offers for nursing can be as high as BBC or 280 tariff points. However, on average, and this applies to Swansea too, candidates require a minimum of 240 UCAS tariff points at A level (typically CCC) or equivalent.

A/AS levels: combination must include two A2 grades

BTEC National Diploma Health Studies: MMM

BTEC Higher Diploma Health Science: Pass

Access to Health/Nursing/Science: 63 level 3 credits (+ key skills)

All applicants need to demonstrate success at study in previous 3–5 years. Although no specific subjects are required it is beneficial to study health or science-related courses. Also, care experience may be beneficial.

In addition, applicants are required to demonstrate evidence of ability to read and comprehend In English or Welsh and to communicate effectively in writing; competency in numeracy and will need to have a Criminal Records Bureau check carried out.

WHAT DOES A GOOD PERSONAL STATEMENT LOOK LIKE?

It is helpful if you can talk about the skills you have developed and demonstrate how these skills may be transferable to nursing, for example, skills in communication, team working, organisation, information technology and leadership. You would also be well advised to be able to justify why you have decided to apply for a particular branch of nursing and to highlight any particular interpersonal skills and positions of responsibility held. It may also be helpful to show how the subjects you studied at A level may be applicable to nursing. If you have care experience you may wish to convey what your learnt from this experience. Many nursing courses are accessed via interview and the information included in the statement will probably be used in this interview.

TOP TIPS FOR A GOOD PERSONAL STATEMENT

1 Attend careers fairs, university open days and/ or arrange to speak with admissions tutors before you start to write your personal statement, so that your statement reflects your understanding of the course you have applied for and the demands of the profession

2 Visit the different schools' websites, which will tell you about the admissions process and the programme of study. You will also pick up tips from each department that you might like to include in your statement

3 Ensure there are no errors of spelling or grammar in your application and check that details are correct

4 Ensure that what you write in your personal statement is clearly expressed

5 Establish your motivation and commitment to study

6 Find out about what nurses do – talk to nurses about the profession, healthcare and nursing roles. If you have, let us know in your statement

7 Keep abreast of topical healthcare or health-related issues, for example infection control, nurse prescribing, obesity,

THINGS TO AVOID

1 Poor presentation of your statement

2 Using text-speak in your application, particularly your personal statement

3 Forgetting to proofread your application and statement.

health policy – you may be asked about current issues at interview

8 Ensure you have a good reason for wanting to follow the course at this university and that this is expressed clearly in the opening paragraph of your statement

9 Remind yourself of your personal statement: your interviewers may ask you about aspects of this.

RECOMMENDED READING AND WEBSITES

- *Careers Uncovered: Nursing and Midwifery:* Richmond: Trotman Publishing, 2006
- The Nursing and Midwifery Council (www.nmc-uk.org)
- Royal College of Nursing (www.rcn.org.uk)
- I am grateful for the support I received from the Nursing department at Swansea University (www.swansea.ac.uk) in the preparation of this profile.

OCEANOGRAPHY

This academic profile was written by an admissions tutor at Southampton University. The information is useful to all applicants, but some of the advice is pertinent to that department in particular.

SUBJECT OVERVIEW

'I walk into our control room, with its panoply of views of the sea. There are the updated global pictures from the remote sensors on satellites, there the evolving maps of subsurface variables, there the charts that show the position and status of all our Slocum scientific platforms, and I am satisfied that we are looking at the ocean more intensely and more deeply than anyone anywhere else.'

HENRY STOMMEL, THE SLOCUM MISSION, 1989

The above statement by Henry Stommel summarises the fundamental changes that oceanography has experienced in the last two decades because of the major advances in marine technology. Studying oceanography involves interdisciplinary studies and research in estuarine, coastal and open-ocean environments. Oceanography includes many scientific fields such as physics, geology, chemistry, biology, meteorology, geography, and geodesy. In addition to oceanography, a broad range of course opportunities are available involving different disciplines and technologies from remote sensing to molecular biology.

Because being an oceanographer is about studying the ocean, most oceanographers spend a great deal of time at sea. During the degree, lectures provide the theoretical background to the subject area, laboratory practicals and field work provide hands-on training in experimental activities and surveying techniques. During the degree, students have the opportunity to conduct real-time studies in coastal waters of the UK and abroad using advanced underwater instrumentation. These involve the application of knowledge acquired in biological, chemical, physical and geological processes, deep-sea biology, satellite technology, ocean modelling, fish biology, ocean optics, biodiversity and marine molecular biology.

All students receive training in professional key skills such scientific writing, oral presentations, and poster presentations, which are key to excel and succeed as a professional oceanographer regardless of the career path the student chooses to take. Being taught by academics who are active researchers, students acquire first-hand learning about the latest developments of oceanography. In summary, this is an exciting time to be an oceanographer!

WHAT SKILLS OR ATTRIBUTES DO ADMISSIONS TUTORS LOOK FOR IN A GOOD APPLICANT?

You should display a drive and enthusiasm for – and an informed understanding of – the degree programme(s) for which you have applied. You should be able to demonstrate that you have thoroughly researched the subject area and have considered why you wish to undertake such a degree in the context of your future career development. You will be expected to have ensured that your academic background and the examinations you have yet to take are acceptable, and that your qualifications will be of a sufficient level of attainment, to ensure admission to the course of their choice.

You should provide sufficient information in your personal statement to indicate that you not only appreciate the personal skills and abilities required for successful completion of an earth science degree, but that you can illustrate such an appreciation with pertinent personal examples in the form of education-based experiences (for example, personal and team-based sporting or musical activities), extracurricular or work experiences. If you can provide evidence or demonstrate well-developed time and personal management skills, English language, grammar and numerical skills, along with a degree of independence, these are all aspects of your character that will be of interest to admissions staff.

WHAT DOES A GOOD PERSONAL STATEMENT LOOK LIKE?

Your personal statement should provide an admissions tutor with sufficient information to convey that you have not only a drive and enthusiasm for the degree programme(s) for which you are applying, but also that you have thoroughly researched the subject area and have considered why you wish to undertake such a degree in the context of your future career development. As a potential applicant you will be expected to tailor your personal statement to address your interest in the wider subject discipline and perhaps in specific areas of the discipline. To realise this you may choose to draw upon your own experiences in AS/A2 level subjects, involvement in subject-related extracurricular activities or work experience. This part of the statement ought to comprise some 30–50% of the whole statement, and should be reflective and demonstrate self-awareness. As all earth and marine science subject areas will have a practical, field-based component, you ought to highlight any such experience and skills which you already have, be it study-based (for example, A levels), or extracurricular (for example, Duke of Edinburgh's Award Scheme, Operation Raleigh, or activity-style holidays you have organised for yourself).

However, many of the personal skills and abilities required for successful completion of an earth or marine science degree can also be demonstrated by reference to other forms of education-based experience (for example, personal and Individual/ team-based sporting or musical activities), or work experience. If you can provide evidence for time and personal management skills and independence, these are all aspects of your character that will be of interest to admissions staff. Avoid meaningless literary quotes or apparent deep thoughtful insights about your chosen topic that you have picked off a website or invented, admission tutors have read most of them already!

Example of a good personal statement

I have always been fascinated by how the different landscapes in our world have been shaped and formed by the physical workings of the planet. I am particularly interested in Oceanography, Physical Geography and the Earth Systems, including plate tectonics. My study of the mechanisms of river and coastal processes has inspired me to research physical and human impact on the environment. The current debate around climate change adds a further dimension to my interests. Will the film 'The Inconvenient Truth' influence future decisions regarding energy consumption and America's new involvement in tackling climate change and greenhouse emissions? I look forward to exploring the political and ethical elements involved in the debate with equally enthusiastic tutors and fellow students.

I have enjoyed developing my teamwork skills on field trips to Lulworth Cove and at Slapton. In Slapton, I collected river data along the river Lemon and examined results with computer models using 'live' data from the field, and then I used theoretical skills to analyse and evaluate these results. I hope that my fieldwork at School will have helped me prepare for university.

A level ICT is helping me use various applications to support my research work in A level Geography and Biology. I really enjoy Biology as, like Geography, is about the evolution, adaptation and development of organisms. Its appeal is that it complements my work of the physical development of the Earth and the human impact upon it.

Completing the Duke of Edinburgh's Bronze, Silver and Gold Awards was physically and mentally challenging. Attaining Grade 4 Flute, playing in the School orchestra, and passing my driving test are some of the varied skills I have enjoyed and acquired. While on the Isle of Arran, I really enjoyed the challenge of studying the environment and how it was shaped by geographical and geological processes.

I am a keen gymnast and I really enjoy sports, in particular tennis, hockey and netball. As part of my community service I qualified as an assistant gymnastics coach. I hope that I can use these skills while at university so that I can be part of the university and the local community.

This year I was elected a school prefect. My subject responsibilities are Geography and Information and Communication Technology. As part of my role as Geography Prefect, I am currently in the process of developing a Geography Society. This will include arranging debates about current geographical issues and organising other activities such as model making and quizzes. I am also involved in helping host the World Wide Quiz for local schools. Other roles include responsibility for Junior School and being Minute Secretary for meetings for the Headmistress and Prefects. I am also part of a team involved in the development of a new school prospectus. I have improved my organisation and communication skills through involvement in school events and working closely with the Parents' Committee at social and fundraising events.

I enjoy travelling and last year I went to Russia with an Irish dance school, visiting Moscow and Perm. This trip gave me the chance to see a different culture and landscape as we travelled through the taiga on the Trans-Siberian Express. The isolated rural villages with few resources were especially interesting and memorable.

I look forward to studying Geography to degree level. I believe I am positive, enthusiastic and able to manage my academic and extracurricular activities, and feel I am well prepared for the challenge of university life and all that it has to offer.

TOP TIPS FOR A GOOD PERSONAL STATEMENT

1 Ensure your qualifications meet published admissions criteria for the particular degree course for which you are applying before you even start to write your personal statement!

THINGS TO AVOID

1 Applying for courses without having checked you have the correct qualifications to offer

2 Using literary quotes, or unlikely and apparently deeply thoughtful insights about your degree subject to try and impress in your personal statement

2 Provide honest and reflective comments about why you wish to study at university and what you want to achieve in your personal statement and pay attention to presentation (for example, checking for correct spelling and grammar).

3 Applying to courses that you do not feel passionate about. This lack of passion is often evident in the personal statement

4 Being careless with the writing of the application, for example, not checking for spelling mistakes, missing information required by the admissions Team. Not being professional is a bad sign for any admissions tutor and any future employer!

RECOMMENDED READING AND WEBSITES

- *New Scientist* (www.newscientist.com)
- *Nature* (www.nature.com)
- *Discover* (www.discovermagazine.com)
- *National Geographic* (www.nationalgeographic.com)
- Royal Geographical Society (www.rgs.org)
- Geological Association (www.geologists.org.uk)
- I am grateful to the Oceanography department at Southampton University (www.soc.soton.ac.uk) for their support in writing this profile.

PERFORMING ARTS

This academic profile was written using information provided by an admissions tutor at Liverpool Institute for the Performing Arts (LIPA). The information is useful to all applicants, but some of the advice is pertinent to LIPA in particular.

SUBJECT OVERVIEW

A degree course in acting not only provides technical training and the building of a secure acting process but also encourages students to think of their work in a broader context and teaches you to plan, prepare, research and adapt, all of which are important for the actor.

WHAT SKILLS OR ATTRIBUTES DO ADMISSIONS TUTORS LOOK FOR IN A GOOD APPLICANT?

Academically, most departments are looking for a person with five GCSE passes at a minimum grade of C or above, normally including English and Maths. In terms of Level 3 qualifications LIPA does not specify which subjects you need to study – we are looking for people who achieve a minimum of 180 UCAS tariff points, which should ideally be attained in one of the following ways

Grade B and C at A level or AVCE level. All A level subjects accepted, excluding General Studies.

Merit, Merit, Pass Profile at BTEC National Diploma level.

All equivalent UK and overseas qualifications are also accepted, including Welsh Baccalaureate, Scottish Highers, Welsh, European and International Baccalaureate and Irish Leaving Certificate.

We are interested in your talent and ability as an actor so a level of experience in acting, preferably in a variety of contexts is definitely something we look for. Your interdisciplinary experience is also important, so we look for your potential to train in a second discipline (for example, directing, singing, dancing). You do not have to be a polished performer – demonstrable potential is equally important. We are also interested in your communication skills and in people who can demonstrate that they are enterprising.

In terms of personality traits, we also look for people who are hungry to learn and can self-manage their learning. A good sense of humour and the ability to work collaboratively are useful traits for an actor. An ability to articulate that you can reflect on your practical experience – whether that is verbally or in writing – is important.

WHAT DOES A GOOD PERSONAL STATEMENT LOOK LIKE?

The most important thing is to communicate a sense of why you think acting is important. The danger is that you write this in a way that comes across as egocentric. While a level of passion should be evident, your statement should support this with examples of relevant experience. An ability to look beyond the most obviously available opportunities (such as the school play) is an additional factor that can help make you stand out. Simply to say that you have always wanted to be an actor or always had a dream to act is not enough. In addition, any experience that suggests engagement with broader social issues can be a positive reinforcement (for example, voluntary work, travel, responsible roles within school or other organisations).

Example from good personal statements

> 'All the world's a stage' Shakespeare once said, and for me this statement is truer than any other. Drama and performing is my passion, ever since a young age my sights have been set on performing at the highest level. Through the years, my desire to achieve my goals of becoming an actress in the West End and to join the Royal Shakespeare Company have become stronger and more focused. I believe that my acceptance into this, one of the leading conservatoires in Britain – if not the world – will be the best starting stepping stone into this highly competitive profession.

✓ This opening paragraph in the applicant's personal statement illustrates her passion for a career in acting and demonstrates her focus.

> I am a member of several different theatre groups and musical theatre companies, doing around three public performances locally every year, plus musical reviews regularly for local charity events and private functions. My membership to one of these groups, also afforded me the invaluable experience of performing in the National Theatre, London, as part of the Youth Theatre Shell Connections Festival in 2003. Therefore, I feel that my performance experience is definitely a strong point. I have also done professional work for television including extras work in the series 'Teachers' on Channel 4, and in a film to be screened around October 2006 called 'Outlaw'.

✓ This paragraph demonstrates that the applicant has experience in a range of contexts and has an understanding of the differences involved in acting in different contexts. She has been doing reviews for local charity events and private functions, which suggests enterprise. And we can only agree with her statement 'therefore I feel that my performance experience is definitely a strong point'. She has clearly made the effort to get herself involved with a lot of acting activities.

> As well as a great interest in drama/theatre and musicals, I am a keen sportswoman, achieving a place in the Welsh development netball squad in 2004, and I have a strong interest in dance and movement, also attaining a trained level of stage combat and movement. Other interests that I have include art, languages, reading and singing. As a musician, I have also achieved Grade 5 singing, Grade 5 in flute and in violin Grade 3. I also have a keen interest in composing and being a lyricist.

✓ This last paragraph demonstrates that she is trainable in more than one discipline (movement and music). She also engages in other forms of social activity, outside of the performing arts, as she identifies her achievements in netball. Stage combat is also relevant to the acting course. Her interest in art, languages and reading suggest an all round general sense of enquiry about the world.

Another candidate says:

> Being a member of two drama companies for five years gave me the experience to broaden my horizons by attaining a speaking part on 'Her Benny', which was held in the Liverpool Empire in 2002. After this I acquired a taste for the stage and knew I wanted to perform professionally on the West End. I went on to further my performing experience in the world of film by working for three years as an extra and had small parts with Mersey Television. Also playing a main role in a short film for trainee purposes helped me improve my skills in front of the camera.

✓ This shows a good breadth of acting experience and also enterprise. The applicant is clearly committed because he has sought out these acting opportunities.

> Working part-time behind the bar at my local sports and social Club and weekends at my local supermarket has improved my communication and social skills, which enables me to interact well with others.

✓ This suggests he is good at managing his time. He must be self-disciplined to manage to fit this work in, on top of his studies. It's also good that he perceived the benefits of improving his communication and social skills.

> I am looking forward to focussing on all aspects of performing arts in more depth, facing new challenges and meeting different people throughout my time at university. I hope to further acquire a variety of skills that will benefit me in life and in my chosen career.

✓ This last paragraph shows his focus and suitability for our course, plus a hunger to learn and recognition about the benefits that come from meeting different people.

TOP TIPS FOR A GOOD PERSONAL STATEMENT

1 The following advice comes in part from a recent LIPA graduate. The advice is good for anyone applying to study acting at any of the major schools, although she studied with us here at LIPA

2 See as much theatre or performance art as possible. Watching with an interested and critical eye helps you in so many ways. If you can look at others with a critical eye, you can also look at yourself in the same way. Make sure that you mention your recent experience in your statement

3 You must be certain that the course you choose to apply for is right for you. Be thorough in your research of the course and institution. You need to do everything you can to be confident in your choices. This confidence in the course should be obvious in your statement – tell the tutor that you have done the right research and know that this is the course for you

4 Sell your achievements in a positive way – do not undersell yourself and where you can mention any performance, production, directing or other relevant experience that you would.

TOP TIPS FOR AUDITIONS

1 Make sure you understand every word of any chosen piece and do not pick these from an 'audition speeches' book

2 Always read around before picking audition speeches and songs

3 Be prepared to talk about anything that you may have mentioned in your statement

4 Dress appropriately – you need to see any audition as a practical job interview so dress appropriately – do not dress in an outfit you would wear for social occasions.

 THINGS TO AVOID

1 Leaving preparation to the last minute – you will not be able to learn that Shakespeare speech on the train to LIPA or any other acting school!

2 Careless errors in your statement

3 Anything that you cannot defend or discuss at interview

4 Copying from another source.

RECOMMENDED READING AND WEBSITES

■ CRAC Degree Course Guide: *Music, Drama and Dance*, Richmond: CRAC/ Trotman Publishing, 2007

■ I am grateful to LIPA (www.lipa.ac.uk) for their assistance in writing this profile.

PHILOSOPHY

This academic profile was written an admissions tutor at King's College, University of London. The information is useful to all applicants, but some of the advice is pertinent to King's in particular.

SUBJECT OVERVIEW

Philosophy is one of the oldest and most fundamental academic disciplines that examine the nature of the universe and humanity's place in it. It explores the essence of mind, language, morality and physical reality, and discusses the methods used to investigate these topics. Studying philosophy at university will give you the chance to get to grips with these themes by reading and discussing what great philosophers have had to say about them and forming your own ideas, at the same time developing your powers of logical and creative thinking.

WHAT SKILLS OR ATTRIBUTES DO ADMISSIONS TUTORS LOOK FOR IN A GOOD APPLICANT?

We are looking for students who enjoy thinking about fundamental questions in a logical way. The ability to express yourself clearly both orally and in writing is important. Students who do well at philosophy tend to be open-minded and able to take and receive criticism freely but fairly. Since philosophy rarely reaches definitive answers to the questions it poses, a sense of curiosity is vital but patience can also be a useful attribute. You do not have to study philosophy formally at school, though we do like to see some evidence of your interest in the subject. Competition for entry is high in many of the best departments. As a result the standard offers are now as high as AAB at King's and similar standard departments.

WHAT DOES A GOOD PERSONAL STATEMENT LOOK LIKE?

The most important thing is that you tell us clearly why you want to study philosophy at university and show us some evidence of your interest in the subject. We need to see some evidence of this in your reading so far. You do not need to have read all the major works and even be particularly expert in any. However, we would hope to see evidence that you have read one of the better general introductions to the subject and one of the more accessible philosopher's works. Plato's *Republic* is a good introductory text, as is Mill's *Utilitarianism.* We hope to read a statement that is clear, concise and precise in its presentation. Philosophy is, after all, a subject that is essentially transmitted orally and on paper. If you are applying for a joint honours degree that is fine as long as we can read about both subjects in your statement.

We are predominantly interested in your academic profile but also keen to hear about your extracurricular pursuits.

TOP TIPS FOR A GOOD PERSONAL STATEMENT

1 Talk about why you are interested in studying philosophy. This should be an obvious point, but a significant number of applicants, particularly those applying for joint degrees, say nothing or very little about why they want to do philosophy

THINGS TO AVOID

1 Supplying lots of unnecessary detail about your hobbies and travel abroad – although foreign travel might be more relevant to applications for other subjects, especially modern languages

2 Telling us at length how wonderful you think philosophy is and/or how passionate you are about it – we like to see

2 Mention a few books on philosophy that you have read, and what you found of value in them. Do not just give a reading list

3 If you are also applying for other subjects, feel free to say so, but don't neglect the first two tips!

4 Break your statement up into sections (not too many), don't write it as one continuous paragraph

5 Write clearly and grammatically, and avoid spelling errors

6 Make sure that you proofread your statement properly and that it flows well.

enthusiasm, but be concise and specific rather than vague and general

3 Using jargon and technical vocabulary that you don't understand, just because it sounds impressive – it may impress your friends (though it may not), but it won't fool an experienced university teacher

4 Explaining at length why you want to do a degree other than the one for which you have applied, or at another institution

5 Boasting – let your achievements speak for themselves

6 Plagiarising your personal statement – a serious error of judgement!

RECOMMENDED READING AND WEBSITES

- Nigel Warburton, *Philosophy: The Basics*, London, Routledge, 2004
- Simon Blackburn, *Think: A Compelling Introduction to Philosophy*, Oxford: Oxford Paperbacks, 2001
- Plato, *The Republic*
- I am grateful to the Philosophy department at King's College, London (www.kcl.ac.uk) for their support in compiling this profile.

PHYSICS

This academic profile was written by an admissions tutor at Bath University and focuses on physics as a single honours discipline. The information is useful to all applicants, but please be aware that some of the advice is pertinent to that department in particular.

SUBJECT OVERVIEW

Physics is the fundamental science; it is concerned with the study of matter, energy and the interactions between them, and it involves the search for the universal principles underlying many, very diverse natural phenomena. It is important, not only as a subject in its own right, but also as an essential element in all other natural sciences, engineering and technology. There is also a great deal of enjoyment and satisfaction to be derived from an understanding of the most recent developments in physics research.

Physics graduates combine sound mathematical and experimental expertise with the ability to grasp new concepts, and are able to apply their expertise to many familiar and unfamiliar challenges. Physics often involves the development of mathematical models of complex behaviour and develops the judgement and imagination necessary to solve problems at an appropriate level of approximation. The development of many other important skills – such as written and verbal communication, computational skills, and teamworking, is embedded in physics degree programmes.

The versatility of physics is reflected in the wide variety of occupations in which they may be found. Nearly all modern industries call on the insight and technical expertise of physicists. Physicists are equally valued for the contribution they can make to education, administration, business and commerce, where their problem-solving skills are in great demand.

WHAT SKILLS OR ATTRIBUTES DO ADMISSIONS TUTORS LOOK FOR IN A GOOD APPLICANT?

The most important attributes are a high level of competence in mathematics and physics, with particular emphasis on the former, and an enthusiasm for the study of physics. Admissions tutors also look for good communication skills, and evidence of ability to work alone or in groups. However, most students exhibit a tremendous diversity of personalities and interests, and we are very pleased that this is the case: anoraks are not required!

WHAT DOES A GOOD PERSONAL STATEMENT LOOK LIKE?

Your statement is going to be read by five admissions tutors from five different departments – so avoid being too specific in stating your interests – for example, not every department offers cosmology options; do not betray your first choice(s); do not say that you have always wanted to be a mathematician if you are applying for both mathematics and physics programmes, or even for joint degree programmes; if you are applying to physics programmes as an alternative to a medical degree, then make this clear in your statement (for example, do not just mention medicine).

We look for good grammatical construction and good motivation. Be original – don't just write what you think you should, and definitely don't download – without being quirky for the sake of it. Anything you write about is fair game if you are interviewed, when you will be expected to be able to talk about anything in your statement – so be honest.

Examples from good personal statements

At Bath, in common with most other physics departments in the country, we pay most attention to academic achievement and potential as contained primarily in A level grades (or equivalent). We rarely reject a student because of a personal statement; in our experience, most statements are written adequately. Any statement written following the guidelines above would be acceptable. However, in the case of a student who has narrowly missed their offer grades, we may look to your statement for signs of something special.

Students generally begin by expressing their interest in and commitment to physics as a discipline, provide some evidence of this – usually in the form of reading matter and short events they have attended – and end with a description of their other activities and interests. Such statements are fine, but generally contain nothing to catch the eye. The following example is good because it is brief, honest and to the point:

> I have chosen to study Physics at university as I want to study a subject that is not only universally useful, but is always crossing new frontiers of knowledge.

✓ A good start, and not too flowery.

> Physics has always interested me.

✓ Cliché alert!

> and I particularly want to continue with it as studying the subject over the years has brought just as many new questions to me as it has answered. I have always tried to keep up to date with scientific developments and as such I read issues of 'New Scientist', and I have currently been reading the Richard Feynman lectures.

✓ This is good because it avoids reference to Stephen Hawking!

> In July 2006 I attended a three day Physics course at XYZ University.

✓ Excellent.

> This was a valuable experience, involving problem solving exercises and sample lectures, which gave me an insight into the areas of physics in which I would be most interested in specialising. Nanoscience is an area that consequently attracted me due to its interdisciplinary nature, as it can be applied to practically everything from electronics and engineering to biology and the environment. I'm sure there will be great progress in this field in the near future.
> I have applied for MPhys/MSci courses as I am keen to pursue a career in research, and as such my shortlist of universities have all been selected for their strong research facilities.

✓ Shows that some research has been done into which choices to make.

> Aside from Mathematics and Physics, I also chose my A levels to cater for analytical skills and to keep up a well-rounded education. Classics was a completely new subject to me and I was interested in taking on something fresh. History provided more breadth to my A levels, and I think it is important to be well informed, particularly on aspects of modern world history. Both of these subjects have the bonus of maintaining my fluency in essay writing.

✓ Evidence of scholarship.

I enjoy music, and I am an avid guitarist. I play acoustic, bass, and particularly electric to a very high standard. I frequently play with others for entertainment and have posted videos of performance on the internet which received very pleasing feedback. I also write music, and aside from my own compositions I am working on a number of joint projects with a friend. My experience of playing the guitar has even come useful in studying the waves part of the A2 Physics syllabus this year, as I found that I had encountered many phenomena such as resonance and standing waves, and had in fact taken advantage of these for musical effect!

✓ Evidence of interests outside school.

In researching courses, I was encouraged to see the large investment currently being made in Physics departments, and I am certain there are many interesting developments in which I can become involved.

✓ Shows evidence of research into his chosen universities.

Examples from poor statements

The next examples are taken from the beginnings of statements representing the vast majority we receive, which are unlikely to catch the eye:

Ever since an early age I have been fascinated by physics, in particular how and why things work and how vast the subject of physics is . . .
Ever since school I have been interested in sciences . . .
Physics has always intrigued me . . .
My interest in Physics was first awakened when I read 'A Brief History of Time' by Stephen Hawking, at the age of 13 . . .
The wonders of earth and space have interested me from an early age . . .
For many years I have been interested in the sciences . . .
I was fascinated by science and maths from my first years at secondary school . . .
From an early age I have wanted to study Physics so that I can attempt to understand the universe around me . . .
When I was a child I always asked why? I'm now 18 and I still do.

Two examples of misdirected statements (applications to read single-subject physics):

I hold a strong desire to study Physics and Philosophy at university.

Since a very young age, I have had a strong desire to become a doctor.

TOP TIPS FOR A GOOD PERSONAL STATEMENT

1 Find out as much about the course as you can so that you can talk about specific elements that interest you, and why, in your personal statement

2 Make sure you have good reasons for applying to your chosen courses and explain these in your statement

3 Try and be original with your opening statement without being quirky. Admissions tutors have to read hundreds of statements so something more unusual is more likely to catch their interest

4 Refer to your A level (or equivalent) courses and demonstrate how these will prepare you for degree level study of Physics

5 Give evidence of other interests and show how these have given you additional skills that will be useful for university level study.

THINGS TO AVOID

1 A poorly constructed statement, full of grammatical errors and clichés

2 Writing fanciful prose, especially in the opening sentence

3 Mentioning specialities not relevant to some of your chosen departments

4 Mentioning your top choice(s) – you may change your mind!

5 Saying you have read Stephen Hawking's *Brief History of Time*. You may well have done this (at least partly!), and this is commendable, but we read this statement in a large fraction of our applications and it has become a kind of cliché which does not lift you above the crowd.

RECOMMENDED READING AND WEBSITES

- Institute of Physics: www.iop.org
- Nexus (www.iop.org/activity/nexus): student wing of the Institute of Physics
- CRAC Degree Course Guide: *Physics and Chemistry*, Richmond: CRAC/Trotman Publishing, 2007
- I am grateful to the University of Bath (www.bath.ac.uk) for their support in compiling this profile.

PHYSIOTHERAPY

This academic profile was written by an admissions tutor at Brighton University. The information in this profile is useful to all applicants, but some of the advice is pertinent to Brighton in particular.

SUBJECT OVERVIEW

Physiotherapy is an absorbing and fascinating way of working with people in a positive way to improve or maintain their health. Physiotherapists work with people mainly through the use of exercise and manual therapies to enhance health. Degree programmes in physiotherapy provide both university experience and the experience of working with people in healthcare settings. The students go into clinical settings to work with qualified physiotherapists and other health professionals, for example, nurses, doctors, and occupational therapists. This balance of academic and work-based learning is excellent preparation for a career in healthcare.

If you think you would enjoy working with people in a health setting there is plenty of scope for you to develop many technical, academic and interpersonal skills. All physiotherapy degrees need to carry eligibility for state registration, enabling graduates to practise as physiotherapists and be approved by the professional body – The Chartered Society of Physiotherapists.

WHAT SKILLS OR ATTRIBUTES DO ADMISSIONS TUTORS LOOK FOR IN A GOOD APPLICANT?

We are looking for enthusiastic people who have a good academic profile from a wide range of educational experiences and who are prepared to learn. We would like to recruit students who are motivated and have made the effort to find out about physiotherapy. We are particularly keen on people who have had the opportunity to observe different aspects of physiotherapy and are able to explain why they are interested in developing a career in the area.

Most good departments will expect a candidate to have at least one science A level (or equivalent) – preferably Biology or Chemistry. Where two sciences are not offered at A2, another is often required at AS.

Entry standards vary, but most departments now make offers of BBB rising to ABB (or their equivalent). The course consists of theory and practice – a large part of the emphasis at the University of Brighton is the acquisition of physiotherapy skills before going on to clinical placements. This would probably be true of other departments in the UK. The styles of teaching are tutorials, practicals, seminars, workshops and lectures – according to what most suits the learning material.

WHAT DOES A GOOD PERSONAL STATEMENT LOOK LIKE?

It is really helpful, if you have observed some physiotherapy sessions, to briefly describe your experience and explain why you would like to study it. You really need to describe something more varied than a personal experience of receiving physiotherapy – which shows that you have made an effort to see different aspects of physiotherapy – or at least have plans to broaden your understanding. Many departments do not look favourably at an overemphasis on sport. Most physiotherapists work in hospital settings and do not get involved in any form of sports-related injury or rehabilitation.

It is always good to hear about your activities beyond the academic, particularly if you are interested in continuing them at university. If you can, try and show a range of interests other than sport. We are interested in music, drama and other extracurricular pursuits, especially if they show evidence of individual leadership or teamwork skills. If you have had a job or done voluntary work make sure you explain something positive about the experience of interacting with people.

Try and find a balance between self-promotion, explaining your recent experiences of work, social activities and school achievements. Overemphasis on any of these elements can skew your statement.

Example of a good personal statement

> I have shadowed a sports physiotherapist and spent time in an NHS hospital, where I shadowed both junior and senior Physiotherapists in all wards; this combined with my own personal research of the career by means of literature and talking with many physiotherapists has served to increase my desire to commit myself to a career as a physiotherapist.

✓ Shows that an effort has been made beyond personal experience and that active research has been made to understand physiotherapy.

> The diversity in roles astounded me, ranging from the intricacies of the hand clinic to the very manual rehabilitation of stroke patients, where constant feed back on posture and walking gait is given. Despite the various techniques employed, several competencies became very evident to me: A physiotherapist is an excellent communicator, problem solving team player who can work holistically with other members of a multidiplomacy team whose goals are to educate and rehabilitate a patient so that they may return to everyday life as speedily and safely as possible.

✓ Shows some well informed opinion.

> Having travelled and met people from many different backgrounds and age groups, I am confident that I now possess the maturity and keenness of mind to undertake a physiotherapy degree and meet with enthusiasm any of the challenges that a career as a Chartered Physiotherapist poses.

✓ A very literate statement could also include more personal information about hobbies.

 ## TOP TIPS FOR A GOOD PERSONAL STATEMENT

1 Indicate early on your passion for the subject with examples to support this interest

2 Show that you are interested in current health issues

3 Tell the tutor about your work experience and contact with physiotherapists. Say what you

 ## THINGS TO AVOID

1 Telling us how much you want to be a nurse/be a doctor/work in the leisure industry!

2 Writing about anything you are not prepared to talk about at interview

3 Writing about sport to the exclusion of all else – many departments do not look favourably at an overemphasis

learnt from this experience and how it helped you to make up your mind to apply

4 Make sure that your science skills are clearly developed in your statement

5 Write a list of things you have done – be specific and pick out the best

6 It is always good to hear about your activities beyond the academic, particularly if you are interested in continuing them at university

7 Try and find a balance between self-promotion, explaining your recent experiences of work, social activities and school achievements. Overemphasis on any of these elements can skew your statement.

on sport. Most physiotherapists work in hospital settings and do not get involved in any form of sports-related injury or rehabilitation

4 Confusing physiotherapy and psychotherapy!

5 Poor spelling, punctuation and grammar – get your statement proofread by a competent teacher or tutor.

RECOMMENDED READING AND WEBSITES

- Reading any current affairs information about health issues and physiotherapy would be good but there are no particular activities other than your natural keenness to pursue a career in physiotherapy. It would make sense to read a book about what it is like to be a physiotherapist; there are a variety on the market that bring the subject to life. The Chartered Society of Physiotherapists has a good website with a range of information that would extend your knowledge of the subject

- *Getting into Physiotherapy Courses*, Richmond: Trotman Publishing, 2008

- The Chartered Society of Physiotherapy (www.csp.org.uk)

- I am grateful to Brighton University (www.brighton.ac.uk) for their support in preparing this profile.

PODIATRY

This academic profile was written by an admissions tutor at Brighton University. The information is useful to all applicants, but some of the advice is pertinent to Brighton in particular.

SUBJECT OVERVIEW

Chiropodists (now often called podiatrists) diagnose and treat abnormalities of the lower limb. They give professional advice on the prevention of foot problems and on proper care of the foot. Patients will be of all ages from infants to the elderly. Working as a podiatrist can be exciting and rewarding because it involves working in a variety of environments with a number of other healthcare professionals and many different groups of patients who have a wide range of podiatric problems. The scope of practice of a podiatrist is often much wider than many people realise. Some examples of this are:

- Children sometimes have pains in their legs or feet as they grow or have problems walking
- People with diabetes may have problems with the circulation or sensation in their feet
- Sportsmen and sportswomen often suffer from injuries to their legs and feet
- Dancers with long hours rehearsing and performing put stress through their feet that can cause injury
- People needing minor surgery – some nail surgery or laser treatment
- People wanting advice – some people do not need treatment but just want advice about footwear or foot health.

To become a practitioner registered by the Health Professional Council, there is a requirement to undertake and pass a three-year full-time honours degree in podiatry. The degree also provides eligibility to apply for membership of the Society of Chiropodists and Podiatrists (www.feetforlife.org).

The course at Brighton (along with others in the UK) includes a minimum of four further weeks of external clinical placement with NHS trusts. Students benefit from the multidisciplinary medical team, specialist hospital ward rounds, outpatient clinics and orthopaedic operating sessions. Short placements are arranged with specialist podiatrists and a variety of allied health professionals so that the student experiences as wide a range of podiatric care as possible.

The podiatry undergraduate programme is very intensive and requires considerable dedication on the part of the student.

WHAT SKILLS OR ATTRIBUTES DO ADMISSIONS TUTORS LOOK FOR IN A GOOD APPLICANT?

The normal minimum entrance requirements are GCSE C or above in English, Mathematics and Science with an additional expectation that the student will, on average, obtain 240 tariff points or above at AS or A2 or equivalent, usually including a science subject. Mature students enter the programme by a variety of routes, the most common being approved standard Access courses. Entrance requirements may differ for courses at other universities.

You should be well motivated to learn and have an enthusiasm to study at degree level. You should also be fully committed to this area of work.

Communication is probably the most important skill a healthcare worker should possess. You should be able to communicate effectively both verbally and in writing. Although you will be helped to develop these skills during the course of your degree, having well developed interpersonal skills will help you in both the practice learning and theoretical aspects of this programme.

The administration of local anaesthesia and the appreciation of mechanics and statistics in podiatry mean that an understanding of mathematics is required to this level.

Computer technology is used extensively in healthcare and it is therefore important that your ICT skills are developed. Basic word processing, spreadsheet and internet search skills are therefore essential on enrolment, while you can develop others such as PowerPoint during the programme.

WHAT DOES A GOOD PERSONAL STATEMENT LOOK LIKE?

Motivation and commitment: Podiatry is a fascinating subject and a stimulating profession and practitioners are privileged to have working relationships with some of the most vulnerable members of our society. You should show an appreciation of the scope of podiatry and the role of the podiatrist within the multidisciplinary healthcare team, and they should be able to indicate that they are fully committed to this area of work.

Interpersonal skills: As communication is probably the most important skill a healthcare worker should possess, you will need to consider how you have demonstrated effective communication in your life. This would ideally be communication to a mixed audience, using a variety of methods, and perhaps even at different levels.

Interest in working and learning as part of a team: Admissions tutors will be looking for skills of working with others towards a shared goal and operating as part of a team. After-school activities such as debating societies and membership of sports teams can be used as examples of this. Other evidence can be drawn from appropriate discussion of previous life experiences.

Dexterity skills: Practical podiatry requires a high level of dexterity. Applications should include their acquisition of these skills, for example the practice of art and craft skills, the playing of a musical instrument, the skills of design and technology.

Example from a good personal statement

The following applicant demonstrated all the qualities our admissions team look for both by the written word and by using specific examples. Her statement was logical in presentation, well written and with a wide vocabulary, and gave consideration to the attributes a healthcare worker should posses.

I have always been captivated by the human body and how it can perform the most complex of tasks without conscious thought. Because of this fascination, I chose to study Human Biology and Psychology at A2 level, as well as Sports Studies at AS. Through these subjects I have been able to learn more about the mechanics of the body and the relationship of body and mind.

✓ She has attempted to link both the human physiology with the working of the brain, demonstrating an appreciation that podiatry is about psychosocial issues, not just biology.

I am also studying AVCE Health and Social Care (6 units). (She could have perhaps made more of this here, but the remainder of her statement illustrates why this was an important statement).
   Having always aspired to a career in healthcare, I have decided to pursue a degree in podiatry. Having researched the subject thoroughly, I find the scope of opportunities within the profession very exciting.

✓ Shows she has actively looked for information, particularly career choices.

Biomechanics is an area that fascinates me. Having enjoyed the academic study of anatomy and physiology in my A levels, I am eager to combine this theory with practical application.

✓ Shows an appreciation that textbook biology needs translating into applied practice.

I am also keen to learn more about the surgical aspect of podiatry.
   As part of my Health and Social Care course I have had the opportunity to take part in a weekly work experience placement at a podiatry clinic. Through this I have been able to gain an invaluable insight into the profession in a clinical environment. I am learning first-hand about the practical and theoretical side of podiatry, which has further confirmed my desire to study this subject.

✓ This demonstrates motivation and commitment, and that she has been exposed to a reasonable scope of practice of a podiatrist.

Outside school I have worked in retail. From this I have gained experience in the real world, undertaking responsibilities and learning to work with a wide range of people. I enjoy meeting and talking with customers, establishing their needs and having the satisfaction of being able to help them. I have won two awards for my customer service skills.

✓ Communication skills are evidenced here, along with the appreciation that healthcare offers a service to a wide audience. She also illustrates her sense of responsibility.

> Working with other employees in a team has hugely improved my communication skills, but I also enjoy the challenge of using my own initiative. This has greatly improved my self-confidence.

✓ Podiatrists work as part of a team, but for much of their practice they have to work in single chair clinics. This applicant is demonstrating an understanding of the importance of both modes of working.

> My interest in human biology drove me to learn first aid. I am now a fully trained volunteer first aider and cadet leader with St John Ambulance. I devote most of my spare time to organising cadet activities and providing fist aid cover at local events.

✓ Here she is not only evidencing her skills in caring, but her ability to deal with accidents and events that could involve blood and other traumatic situations. She is also communicating that she has a sense of moral obligation and a strong work ethic, that she can cope with stress, has energy and can organise herself and other people.

> Due to the nature of the work I have to communicate effectively and sensitively with a cross-section of people, often in highly stressful situations. I love the work I do and get a great satisfaction from being involved in something so rewarding.
> I can play the piano and have recently taken my Grade 8. In my spare time I like to listen to music and read novels. Jane Eyre is a particular favourite of mine.

✓ Dexterity skills are shown here, along with a rounded approach to life.

> From the experiences I have gained I believe that podiatry is not only the subject I will thoroughly enjoy studying, but that it will provide me with a rewarding long-term career.

 ## TOP TIPS FOR A GOOD PERSONAL STATEMENT

1 Your enthusiasm for the subject should be clear in the opening paragraph. Think about ways in this enthusiasm can be transmitted. If at all possible,

 ## THINGS TO AVOID

1 Not being sure what podiatry is – before you apply make sure that you read up about the subject – indicate this level of research in your statement

2 Mumbling at interview

arrange to meet a practising podiatrist and include what you learnt from this meeting in your statement – this will give you a real edge

2 The tutors expect to see a well written statement that shows off your ability to communicate well. Elsewhere they need to see evidence of your ability to work in teams and communicate effectively to others orally

3 An engaging personality should come across in your statement and later at interview

4 Manual dexterity is a vital part of the assessment process, any evidence you can provide of an ability to use your hands to make, repair or design will be welcome

5 Show that you have a rounded approach to life, including studies – tell tutors about your interests, particularly those that include a need for independence, initiative and teamwork.

3 Failing to support or develop points made in your statement at interview

4 Poor spelling, punctuation and grammar

5 A statement that is uninspiring, lacking in detail about your skills and desire to study this particular vocation.

RECOMMENDED READING AND WEBSITES

▪ Chartered Society of Podiatrists www.feetforlife.org.

PSYCHOLOGY

This academic profile was written by an admissions tutor at Nottingham University. The information is useful to all applicants, but some of the advice is pertinent to that department in particular.

 ## SUBJECT OVERVIEW

A degree in psychology, as well as being extremely interesting, provides a very wide range of employment prospects to its graduates. Modern psychology is a genuine science in its infancy, trying to understand one of the most fascinating systems ever – the human mind. It is a little like studying physics in the days when gravity was just being understood; the field is changing all the time and is rich with new questions to be answered.

Many students (including those who have taken the subject at A level) are surprised about how much of a modern psychology degree concerns experiments testing rigorous hypotheses and studies of brain processes, but they usually learn to appreciate the need for solid data-based theories.

 ## WHAT SKILLS OR ATTRIBUTES DO ADMISSIONS TUTORS LOOK FOR IN A GOOD APPLICANT?

As a multidisciplinary subject, few subject specific skills are required to make a good candidate, other than logical reasoning and the ability to learn. Some of our students come from pure arts backgrounds and really excel at the essay writing, some come from pure science and are very strong in the experimental and analytical components and some have multidisciplinary backgrounds. We find that any combination can work very well. We do normally expect candidates' subjects to be broadly academic – psychology is no soft option at university level and we do want to know that students have developed some of the above skills during their sixth-form period.

In terms of personality, the best students are usually just dedicated and keen. Students who can focus their minds on the task at hand and push themselves will do well. Often that comes down to the fact that they find the subject interesting and are more willing to work hard at it. Psychology students are often outgoing and dynamic but these personal attributes are certainly not necessary for successful selection.

University life is very different from school. There is a much bigger drive to encourage 'autonomous learning' in students, fostering the ability to explore topics themselves. Formal teaching is often in much larger groups – lectures may have several hundred students – and is aimed more at providing the initial basis for the students' learning rather than providing the entire syllabus. Some universities still talk about 'reading for a degree', reflecting the greater amount of time spent in libraries than classes.

WHAT DOES A GOOD PERSONAL STATEMENT LOOK LIKE?

Think about your target audience – the admissions tutor. That person's job is to try and work out whether or not you will perform well on his/her course.

You need to show that a) you know a little about the subject and b) you really want to study it. These are good indicators of your dedication to the course because if you enjoy the material you are keener to work on it. You might show this in different ways; you might want to explain *why* you are interested in the course if there is some compelling reason that you have always been fascinated by the discipline. You might be able to use evidence of additional work or reading that you have carried out in the topic or demonstrate your knowledge of the subject. Obviously, either of these routes should refer to real aspects of contemporary psychology. Reading a psychology journal will stand you in better stead than owning the boxed set of *Cracker*.

One problem for the admissions tutor is trying to work out how generous you are being with the truth. According to most personal statements and references or students are all confident, independent, sociable, intellectual types with excellent debating skills. In reality some students are terrified, some are not very keen to question and some are at university because they didn't want to get a job yet. The difficulty can be in working out which students are which. You can help here by *showing* your skills rather than explaining them. Some students will tell us that they subscribe to *Psychological Bulletin*, but others will discuss a psychological issue that they find interesting. By discussing the issue accurately they demonstrate their interest in a way that is harder to fake, which saves the admissions tutor worrying whether it is a lie.

Extracurricular activities may help to show your ability to achieve your goals and your ability to manage your time (if combined with good grades) but do not go overboard. In particular, do not spend a great deal of time describing pastimes that are not likely to make you a better student. At the end of the day an admissions tutor will be more interested in how well you got through the course than your love of film or your social charisma. We also want to see a wide variety of personalities. Imagine a department where *everyone* was gregarious and confident – it would be painful!

Also bear in mind that the way you write your statement is going to be direct evidence for the admissions tutor of how well you write. Make sure your statement is clear, expressive and accurate. Read through it several times and get someone else to read it. If your personal statement is littered with errors an admissions tutor will not believe the reference when it discusses your excellent essay-writing skills.

Your personal statement is also a time to discuss anything unusual about your qualifications so far. We might be interested in students whose grades haven't previously been as good as they should if they have a convincing explanation that this will change. Some students thrive at university while others suffer from the independent style of learning. Dedication to the course goes a long way. Also, students who have chosen unusual, or less academic, subjects can use this space to explain what the subject is or how it has been beneficial to them in preparing for a psychology degree. Bear in mind that a university lecturer might not realise how much essay writing you had to do, or how much maths is involved in your particular course. The basic *skills* you develop in your sixth form are at least as useful as the specific *knowledge* you have, so English and maths are likely to be at least as useful subjects to take as psychology itself.

Examples from good personal statements

The following student was taking History, Music and Biology A levels as well as General Studies and an AS level in French. Although she has never studied psychology formally, she demonstrates her enthusiasm for the subject throughout her personal statement and shows a great deal of energy in both her work and extracurricular pursuits. The statement is written clearly and carefully with appropriate and error-free language. We can have little doubt that the candidate possesses the necessary academic skills, as well as work ethic, to progress very well at university.

> Psychology strikes me as the most fascinating area of study imaginable. I love the fact that it is such a diverse subject, ranging from animal behaviour or inter-group relations to child psychology and research methodology. I am particularly intrigued by developmental psychology, especially abnormal psychology in children, and I am keen to learn more about the ways in which an application of this subject can benefit children with conditions such as autism.

✓ This shows understanding of what a diverse range of subjects modern psychology covers.

> Through my work as a volunteer with special needs children on summer schemes I have begun to understand more about how autistic children discover and learn, and also how a response to their need for solitude, repetition and a strict routine can often bring them great comfort. I have started to learn sign language and other forms of non-verbal communication, such as PECS, to use in stressful situations where speech may be ineffective. In addition, this work has enabled me to develop my ability to take responsibility, often in demanding situations, and to adapt quickly to difficult circumstances, such as relating to a child whose only form of communication is through spitting. I also enjoyed taking sole care of severely disabled children both in hydrotherapy pools and a sensory room. I have read a number of books including 'The Man Who Mistook His Wife For A Hat' (Oliver Sacks) and have found 'Abnormal Psychology' (Davison and Neal) useful for reference. I particularly liked Margaret Donaldson's 'Children's Minds', as I found Donaldson's criticism of Piaget's theories interesting. Through researching different developmental disorders I was able to gain a better understanding of the individual needs of the children with whom I worked.

✓ She has read around the subject despite not taking any formal course in it and demonstrates that she has read it by discussing the material.

> This both enhanced my ability to interact successfully with the children and fuelled my desire to learn and research more on this topic.
> I enjoy reading about current issues in psychology, for example the latest ideas on the 'nature versus nurture' debate. This is reflected in my A level choices of Biology, which I feel represents the neurological reasons for actions and personality, and History, which shows how past experiences influence decisions and behaviours.

✓ Explaining your choices of A level subjects is good. Actually, this candidate might have been better to emphasise the skills developed during these courses (in history she will have developed her written fluency) rather than the pointing out specific information that has been learned (that behaviour is shaped by previous experience). The skills will be more useful since and take much longer to develop

> Music is a passion of mine; I love the teamwork involved in playing in a group as well as the challenge and discipline involved in mastering new pieces. I recently gained Grade 8 clarinet with distinction and I also play both violin and piano. I am a member of many different orchestras and ensembles. In the main college orchestra I was leader of the second violins and now lead the clarinet section, and these roles have enabled me to develop and improve my leadership skills. I was one of 16 students in the county awarded a place on the Hampshire Specialist Music Course, which has involved participation in many performances throughout the year and has enhanced my ability to manage my time effectively between music practice and academic work.
>
> In my spare time I have organised and led meetings in my school's theological society and evenings for teenagers at my local youth group, and I have worked full days as a childminder for up to four children at a time. This has helped me to appreciate the endurance and creativity needed to stimulate children in an appropriate way for prolonged periods.

✓ You will be very busy at university. Show, if you can, that you have energy and good time management.

TOP TIPS FOR A GOOD PERSONAL STATEMENT

1 Show that a) you know a little about the subject and b) you really want to study it. These are good indicators of your dedication to the course because if you enjoy the material you are keener to work on the more difficult aspects of it

2 Look at exactly what is taught in the department you are

THINGS TO AVOID

1 Discussing, at length, extracurricular activities that do not make you a better student – we want to take rounded students but stick to the activities that add value to your application in your statement – don't just list them!

2 Claiming to be widely read on the subject if you actually know little about it – this is often clear when reading the statement and applying to and make sure that you indicate somewhere in your statement that you have done this important research

3 Check your form and statement for errors carefully – get your statement proofread by someone you trust

4 *Show* your skills rather than explain them. Some students will tell us that they subscribe to *Psychological Bulletin*, but others will discuss a psychological issue that they find interesting. By discussing the issue accurately they demonstrate their interest in a way that is harder to fake, which saves the admissions tutor worrying if it is a lie.

will become clearer if you are called for interview

3 Forgetting for whom you are writing your statement – an admissions tutor (generally a lecturer in the department)

4 Using slang, text-speak or off-the-wall humour.

RECOMMENDED READING AND WEBSITES

- CRAC Degree Course Guide: *Psychology, Philosophy and Linguistics*, Richmond: CRAC/Trotman Publishing, 2006
- I am grateful for the support I received from the Psychology department at Nottingham (www.nottingham.ac.uk) in the preparation of this profile.

THEATRE AND PERFORMANCE DESIGN AND TECHNOLOGY

This academic profile was written by admissions tutors at the Liverpool Institute of Performing Arts (LIPA). The information is useful to all applicants, but some of the advice is pertinent to that department in particular.

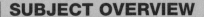

SUBJECT OVERVIEW

The theatre and entertainments industries have a lot of employees who have never studied at university and some areas, like the live sound industry, are keen that all new staff start at the bottom and work their way up, so why would you want to study a degree before starting employment? At university, you should learn a broad base of skills as a technician or designer to give you the flexibility to work in a number of environments, whereas an employer might initially want you for a specific task and not give you the opportunities to try new tasks. You may not need to start at the very bottom as a graduate, and you are much more likely to rise a lot faster even if you do. You may also hit a 'glass ceiling' as a non-graduate where some organisations will only offer their more senior positions to applicants with a degree.

WHAT SKILLS OR ATTRIBUTES DO ADMISSIONS TUTORS LOOK FOR IN A GOOD APPLICANT?

Academically, we are looking for people with five GCSE passes at a minimum grade of C or above, including English. In terms of Level 3 qualifications we don't specify which subjects you need to study – we are looking for people who achieve a minimum of 160 UCAS tariff points, which should ideally be attained in one of the following ways

Grade C and C at A level or AVCE level. All A level subjects accepted, excluding General Studies

Merit, Pass, Pass Profile at BTEC National Diploma level

All equivalent UK and overseas qualifications are also accepted, including Welsh Baccalaureate, Scottish Highers, Welsh, European and International Baccalaureate and Irish Leaving Certificate

These requirements will differ depending on the university and course.

For the design degree, we normally expect applicants to also successfully complete a foundation studies course in art and design or an equivalent course at pre-degree level.

We are also interested in your experience to date in the subject, your interdisciplinary interest, your communication skills and enterprise.

In terms of personality traits, we look for people who are excited about studying the subject. A hunger to learn more and keep learning as your career goes on is important to us. You do not necessarily have to be an expert because if you are you may have nothing left to learn. You need to be good at talking about your own experience and what you have learnt from it and good at analysing your own strengths and weaknesses. You do not have to be perfect – what could we add to that?

A good sense of humour helps – you can be working for long hours, often under pressure with lots of different personalities.

You do not have to be a show-off but you must not be afraid to speak your mind. You will need some kind of independence to take on this degree course and must not be afraid to ask questions if you do not understand something (much better than pretending that you do know something when you don't).

You do not have to be a happy, smiley person about everything – but if you come in and complain about the course you're on at the moment or things you have done in the past – you may come across as a negative person who may struggle to enjoy anything.

Your enthusiasm should show itself in being able to describe what you like in a variety of different ways.

WHAT DOES A GOOD PERSONAL STATEMENT LOOK LIKE?

You need to show enthusiasm, coupled with a clear idea of where you want to go in the future and why this type of course might help you get there or narrow down your choices. It would help if you explain why studying at university is important as well as why you just want to study the subject itself.

Example from a good personal statement

At the moment I'm on an Art and Foundation course and have a big interest in 3-D design and often try to combine my techniques from all areas, using my knowledge of structure to design and make extravagant garments. I especially enjoy working on combining materials such as wire, metal and wood with fabric. I have learnt how to manipulate material in different ways. I like experimenting with different techniques to produce different looks. I have had the opportunity to work in a wide variety of materials and styles and have been encouraged to be more creative and independent in my work. In my courses I particularly enjoy 'realisation', where I actually make my final design. It is the most exciting section of the coursework. And also the design process where I illustrate and explore media to record ideas. It is very satisfying when you can see how you have come to produce this final item. I find contextual studies very interesting as I get a chance to explore and admire other artists' work, observing how their work relates to things around us. During these last two years of my studies I have built up a knowledge of other artists, in particular in my third year I have begun to create a personal sketch book of information and creativity of artists whose work inspires me by visiting galleries and other sources.

In this statement, the applicant describes what s/he is doing now with enthusiasm and talks about developing these skills further in ways that are relevant to our course.

One of the main reasons why a personal statement might not work for us, would be if the candidate appears to be torn between two different career paths. For example, if you are applying to acting or directing courses and are also applying to a design/technology course that suggests you might not be all that committed to our course. Being a designer or technician is a career in itself and we want to know you are committed to that – not to see it as a pathway to a career in performing. In one personal statement someone commented that they were really looking forward to 'retail display design'. This is not the course that they are applying for at LIPA. Similarly another candidate spoke about their love of teaching and the fact that they really want to work with primary school children. That is not part of our course so that candidate is more likely to be better placed studying a focused educational degree. We do have some students whose career aspirations change while studying but if you already know before starting university that you'd rather do something else then that's what you should be looking for in the courses you apply to.

TOP TIPS FOR A GOOD PERSONAL STATEMENT

These tips are from a student who is studying Theatre and Performance Design at LIPA:

1 Get involved both in school and outside of school if you can (try to explore opportunities to take part in local theatre) – this will enable you to write about these experiences in the personal statement and sell your genuine interest in the subject

2 Talk to people – both those who work on stage and backstage, about what happens behind the scenes. Their experiences and what you learnt from them can also provide vital evidence of your interest. Put this in your statement

3 Try everything once – even if you don't carry on working on that element of the production in the future. Being able to understand everything that goes on in a theatre helps in the future. This willingness to try and not being afraid to ask is something that you should allude to the statement and any interview you may be asked to attend

4 Watch shows and performances – that is what you will work towards, so it is always good and satisfying to see the final results. If you see a show

THINGS TO AVOID

1 Complaining that you haven't had any opportunities up till now – life is what you make it! A good personal statement needs to reflect the fact that you have seen productions and done interesting things, so start now!

2 Thinking that musical theatre in the West End is the only successful or interesting type of show going on

3 Being an anorak – having a passion for something is more relevant to us than knowing every serial number or model number

4 Concentrating your design work into fashionable or niche areas such as pictures of fairies or angels – try and show a breadth of your interest and a range of different applications in the statement or portfolio you bring to university

5 Poor spelling, grammar and punctuation. This is just lazy and shows that you are not really serious. If in doubt, get your statement and application proofread by a good teacher, tutor or friend.

and want to comment about the set design in the statement, this would be good.

5 Draw, take photos and keep your show programmes. Keep a record of everything you do, otherwise you have got nothing to show for it. Bring this to any interview you may have.

RECOMMENDED READING AND WEBSITES

- Gary Thorne, *Stage Design: A Practical Guide*, Marlborough: Crowood Press, 1999
- I am grateful for the support I received from LIPA (www.lipa.ac.uk) in the preparation of this profile.

TOURISM MANAGEMENT

This academic profile was written an admissions tutor at Surrey University. The information is useful to all applicants, but some of the advice is pertinent to Surrey in particular.

SUBJECT OVERVIEW

Tourism is an activity of increasing economic activity in the world and makes important contributions to Gross National Product (GNP), employment, foreign currency earnings and employment. It also has both positive and negative social and environmental impacts and can contribute to poverty reduction. Because of this, universities have increasingly become interested in the management and understanding of tourism.

WHAT SKILLS OR ATTRIBUTES DO ADMISSIONS TUTORS LOOK FOR IN A GOOD APPLICANT?

There are no specific academic subjects that are prerequisites for studying tourism. More important are an interest and passion for the subject and evidence that you can benefit from a university course. The industry stereotype is for extrovert, fun-loving personality types – but there are also many opportunities for more introverted studious applicants!

Clearly the teaching styles will vary from department to department, however at Surrey we would expect to offer contact time of between 12–18 hours per week. As the subject is relatively new, teaching and learning styles tend to be dynamic and innovative. Many courses include a field trip abroad. Assessment is generally mixed including exams, coursework, projects and group work.

WHAT DOES A GOOD PERSONAL STATEMENT LOOK LIKE?

A good personal statement has a clear structure with an introduction, a number of clearly explained and relevant points and a conclusion. It is well written, with correct grammar and spelling and without repetition. It effectively links your background, achievements, experience and interests to the course for which you have applied and it shows that you have undertaken some research into the subject area and into the nature of education at university level. It also shows that you have wider interests and achievements than those solely related to the course for which you have applied, and ideally you should show that you have critical and analytical abilities.

With these in mind the structure is likely to include:
- Information about you and your interests and ambitions
- Your present studies and how these relate to your study and longer-term ambitions
- Your particular achievements
- Your broad understanding and knowledge of your planned field of study

- Why you are interested in it
- How you feel you would contribute to the field
- Critical awareness of an issue or issues related to tourism and an ability to analyse the issue.

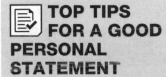 **TOP TIPS FOR A GOOD PERSONAL STATEMENT**

1 Make sure that your statement has a clear structure with an introduction, a number of clearly explained and relevant points and a conclusion

2 Have clear goals and make them clear in your statement

3 Your statement must be well written, with correct grammar and spelling and without repetition

4 Link your background, achievements, experience and interests to the course for which you have applied, and show that you have undertaken some research into the subject area and into the nature of education at university level

5 You must also show that you have wider interests and achievements than those solely related to the course for which you have applied and ideally you should show that you have critical and analytical abilities

 THINGS TO AVOID

1 Poor spelling, punctuation and grammar

2 A statement that lacks clarity and direction

3 A statement that does not refer to your academic skills and extracurricular interests

4 A statement that shows little evidence of an understanding of business and the tourism industry in general

RECOMMENDED READING AND WEBSITES

- The Tourism Society (www.tourismsociety.org)
- I am grateful to the department at the University of Surrey (www.surrey .ac.uk) for their support in compiling this profile.

VETERINARY SCIENCE

This academic profile was written by an admissions tutor at Nottingham University Veterinary School, which is newest of all the schools, having opened in 2006. The information is pertinent to all applicants but please be aware that some advice is relevant to this department alone.

SUBJECT OVERVIEW

Studying veterinary medicine and science will allow you to gain the professionally recognised qualification, which will allow you to practise as a veterinary surgeon. Making the decision to become a veterinary surgeon will set you on a course for one of the most varied and exciting careers available. The veterinary profession offers many diverse and stimulating career opportunities combined with the privilege of working with animals.

Only six institutions offer veterinary medicine in the UK – Bristol, Cambridge, Edinburgh, Glasgow, Liverpool, London (Royal Veterinary College) and Nottingham. Competition is high, but it is a myth that you need to be exceptionally academic.

WHAT SKILLS OR ATTRIBUTES DO ADMISSIONS TUTORS LOOK FOR IN A GOOD APPLICANT?

Academically you should be able to show good overall achievement at GCSE level, including high grades in science subjects. At A2 level, normally most vet schools would expect students to have studied biology and chemistry, and be able to achieve high grades in these subjects. There are now other entry routes into vet school including the preliminary year at Nottingham (which accepts students with high grades in non-science or vocational subjects). There are also widening participation courses specifically aimed at learners from underrepresented groups, such as the Gateway course run at RVC and Veterinary Science Certificate course at Lincoln (for progression to Nottingham) – these courses generally look for grades CCC at A2 level.

As a vet you will need good communication skills – listening, writing and speaking and motor skills such as good hand-eye co-ordination, dexterity and precision of motor skills. All vet schools will expect that you have gained some animal-focused work experience, preferably in a range of animal-related areas such as at a veterinary practice, working with horses or on a farm, at a zoo or wildlife park, in research or laboratory settings and spending time at an abattoir. You would be expected to have an understanding of the positive and negative aspects of a veterinary career and have an awareness of current important issues and developments in veterinary medicine and science.

It is important that you possess a number of personal attitudes and attributes that are needed to both be successful on the course and in a veterinary career including a caring ethos (compassion, tolerance, patience, empathy) and a sense of social responsibility. You should be able to cope with change and uncertainty and to overcome challenges while understanding your own limitations. Schools expect applicants to possess self-motivation, self-confidence, self-reliance and initiative. You should be able to show that you have the ability to work independently and as part of a team, integrate, co-operate and be flexible. Good personal organisational skills and time management skills are a must.

WHAT DOES A GOOD PERSONAL STATEMENT LOOK LIKE?

A good personal statement will cover why you want to study veterinary medicine and science, detail your experience gained to date and your understanding of the profession. Admissions tutors would like to see some evidence of work experience where you came into contact with animals.

This needs to be at least two weeks in length and references may be taken. Taster courses such as VETSIX are popular, useful but not obligatory. Mention the aspects of your A levels (or equivalent) that you have found particularly interesting. Describe any coursework you have completed and any books that you have read that may be relevant. Please do not lie, as this will become clear at interview!

Your statement should cover personal responsibilities and leadership, and any achievements and awards won, and an indication of how these relate to competences required of a veterinary surgeon. Needless to say structure and organisation, grammar and spelling are also important.

Although your personal statement is important, most schools will have additional methods of assessment including the Biomedical Admissions Test (BMAT – www.bmat.org), online questionnaires and work experience references.

TOP TIPS FOR A GOOD PERSONAL STATEMENT

1 Say why you want to study veterinary medicine and science

2 Detail your experience gained to date and your understanding of the profession

3 Emphasise the work experience early on and explain what you learnt as well as what you did

4 Taster courses such as VETSIX are popular and useful – but not obligatory

5 Mention the aspects of your A levels (or equivalent) that you have found particularly interesting

THINGS TO AVOID

1 Having a rose-tinted picture of the profession – it will include working at night, in all conditions and you will be paid as much as a medic! Show that you understand this in your statement and interview

2 Poor spelling, grammar and punctuation.

6 Include personal responsibilities and leadership, and any achievements and awards won, and an indication of how these relate to the competences required of a veterinary surgeon.

RECOMMENDED READING AND WEBSITES

- Royal College of Veterinary Surgeons (www.rcvs.org.uk) produces a free leaflet called *Training to become a veterinary surgeon*
- I am grateful to Nottingham University Veterinary School (www.nottingham .ac.uk/vet) for their support in compiling this profile.

Here are some excellent books, journals or websites that you might like to use to help with your research. This is not an exhaustive list. New books are written and websites created every month. These are the ones that I have found most helpful and they are all currently on sale or available online.

GOOD UNIVERSITY GUIDES

There are many of these guides in the bookshops. Some are better than others and below you will find my personal top five that ought to be in every library. If not, ask for them to be bought or get hold of one of them for your own use!

The Guardian University Guide
Guardian Books
Packed with no-nonsense advice, the *Guardian University Guide* takes prospective students through every process they will encounter when entering further education. It is updated annually and the subject ratings are up to date and based on the UCAS tariff.

The Times Good University Guide
Times Books
This is also updated annually and went online in 2008. Although formal in style it does offer sound and unbiased advice. It also has a league table to help differentiate between the quality of departments in the various universities and colleges.

The Virgin Alternative Guide to British Universities
Virgin Books
This guide was favourably reviewed by the *Times Educational Supplement* and *Careers Advisers Magazine*. It is written in a more informal style with regular contributions from real students. As well as offering a comprehensive guide to all the major UK universities, it also looks at aspects of student life that other sources ignore. For instance, the reader can find out where the students can get the best discounts, the best pubs and where to go to get the best second hand books.

Push Guide to Which University
Hodder Education
This is another interesting guide to university life. Like the Virgin guide, it is written in an informal style. This guide is written by recent undergraduates, who as a result, are well placed to provide frank advice to would-be undergraduates.

Student Book

Trotman

This book is another informative guide that contains over 250 university and college profiles. It provides candid information about all of the major issues that interest potential students including, tuition fees, accommodation, the availability of bursaries, the graduate employment statistics, male/female ratio, the quality of the student union and the best place to buy a curry.

ALTERNATIVE GUIDES

Many universities now produce alternative prospectuses and guides. These are written by students, for students and are not always endorsed by the college authorities. While they will promote the university, they do offer an insight into the day-to-day life of a student that you will not find elsewhere.

Most of these guides are available online. You can usually find them in Google or Yahoo using the search words.

However, one site that offers a 'one stop shop' approach is www.whatuni.com, where current students post comments about the university where they are studying.

GENERAL GUIDES TO SUBJECTS AND COURSE REQUIREMENTS

UCAS Big Guide

UCAS (updated annually – available as a book and CD Rom)

This book and CD-ROM package is the only guide to contain complete entry requirements for all UK higher education courses using the UCAS tariff. The *Big Guide* forms an important part of your research and can be used in all stages leading up to the completion of your UCAS application.

Degree Course Offers

Trotman Publishing

This book is one of the best known in the higher education world. Edited by Brian Heap, it is annually updated and provides the most comprehensive single source for subject specific information available. Students can find out research a range of subjects, including offers most commonly made in each university, information about interviews, open days and the number of applicants who apply per place.

Getting into course guides
Trotman Publishing

Each title in this series, which is updated regularly, provides an unbiased and frank insight into what it is like to study each subject at university, how to impress at interview, current issues that are pertinent to the subject and advice about which university to choose.

The range of titles on offer includes Art and Design, Law, Medicine, Physiotherapy, Psychology and Business Management.

Green Guides: Art, Design and Performing Arts Courses
Trotman Publishing

This guide to art, design and performing arts courses is first class and well worth investing in. The information is current, attractively displayed and written in a style that is appealing to both the student and tutor.

CRAC/Trotman Degree Course Guides
Trotman Publishing

This is another well-written series that provides an ideal starting point for research. The guides provide plenty of useful information to help students compare and contrast different subjects and draw up their shortlist.

Art and Design Directory
Inspiring Futures Foundation

This is the best guide to all the Art and Design foundation courses in the UK bar none. It also provides a comprehensive guide to all the undergraduate programmes. This is not a book written for students. Rather it is a book written to provide careers advisors and art school teachers with a definitive source of information. A must but as it is expensive I would keep an eye on it!

Disabled Student's Guide to University
Trotman Publishing

This guide has been written for students with disabilities who are considering higher education. It is thorough in its approach and answers most of the questions that students in this position will ask.

Getting into Oxford and Cambridge
Trotman Publishing
This is a well-written book that offers the potential Oxbridge applicant an insight into the world of Oxford and Cambridge. It contains detailed advice on all the undergraduate colleges and courses and how to decide which to apply for. It explains that application procedure clearly, debunks the myths that persist and offers an insight into the interviews that seem to lie at the heart of most people's concern. It does not attempt to pretend that there is some secret code that you need to learn to win a place.

In my experience, the candidates who win a place from my school tend to be those who are first-class, straight A-grade academics who are obsessively passionate about their subject. Bright sixth formers do not always demonstrate a passion for a subject to an admissions tutor, which is why, so often, they fail to receive a conditional offer. The days of getting in because your parents and grandparents went to the same institution are essentially over.

WEBSITES
General education
These are websites whose aim it is to provide information to students starting out on their journey towards a successful UCAS or CUKAS application. These are all currently available online and their content evolves on a daily basis.

Hot Courses
www.hotcourses.com
A good search engine for courses at university and college.

Push Online
www.push.co.uk
This is the main Push site and well worth a visit.

Centigrade
COA www.coa.co.uk/centigrade
COA is a leading provider of careers and higher education information to school and colleges in the UK and overseas. Its Centigrade programme is endorsed by UCAS and used by many schools as a test to match student's interests

with higher education courses. The test can now be conducted online and the student will receive a report and copy of the COA Careers Directory.

UCAS

www.ucas.ac.uk

The UCAS website remains the primary portal of choice for students. The site has developed significantly in the last few years and now offers a diverse range of research tools. The most obvious is the Course Search function leading to the UCAS Entry Profiles. It also has a free questionnaire produced by COA called the Stamford Test. This is a slimmed down version of Centigrade and one of the activities in this publication involves students undertaking this test.

CUKAS

www.cukas.ac.uk

This is a relatively new site that is managed by UCAS. Conservatoires UK Admissions Service (CUKAS) is the music conservatoire equivalent of UCAS. Currently the following conservatoires accept applications through this online method.

- Birmingham Conservatoire   www.conservatoire.uce.ac.uk
- Leeds College of Music   www.lcm.ac.uk
- Royal College of Music   www.rcm.ac.uk
- Royal Northern College of Music   www.rncm.ac.uk
- Royal Scottish Academy of Music and Drama   www.rsamd.ac.uk
- Royal Welsh College of Music and Drama   www.rwcmd.ac.uk
- Trinity College of Music   www.tcm.ac.uk

Newspapers

Other excellent sources of general information available online include the two best newspaper education sites – *Guardian Education* (www.education. guardian.co.uk) and *Times Online* (www.timesonline.co.uk)

Both provide excellent information that ranks universities and departments according to a range of criteria. As with all league tables they need to be treated with caution. However, they are free and well respected by the careers staff that I meet.